The Staff of Moses

Book 2 - The Apostolic Field Guide Series

Colette Toach

www.ami-bookshop.com

The Staff of Moses
Book 2 - The Apostolic Field Guide Series

ISBN-10: 1-62664-176-5
ISBN-13: 978-1-62664-176-1

Copyright © **2017** by Apostolic Movement International, LLC.
All rights reserved
5663 Balboa Ave #416,
San Diego,
California 92111,
United States of America

1st Printing July 2017

Published by **Apostolic Movement International, LLC**
E-mail Address: admin@ami-bookshop.com
Web Address: www.ami-bookshop.com

All rights reserved under International Copyright Law.
Contents may not be reproduced in whole or in part in any form without the express written consent of the publisher.

Unless specified, all Scripture references taken from the New King James Version®.
Copyright © 1982 by Thomas Nelson. Used by permission. All rights reserved.

Contents

- Contents 3
- Chapter 01 – Defining Moses 10
  - Definition of the Word – Mandate 12
  - 1. Called From Birth 13
  - 2. Sent on a Different Journey (Grew up in Pharaoh's Household) 14
  - 3. A Passion to do Things Right (Although not Always in Wisdom) 17
  - 4. Learning to Serve 18
  - 5. Waiting on God's People to Become Ready 20
  - 6. Multi-faceted Calling 22
- Chapter 02 – The Moses Apostle 26
  - Step 1. Confronting Pharaoh 26
  - Step 2. Set the Captives Free 28
  - Step 3. To Train and Equip 29
  - Step 4. Raise up Leaders 30
  - Step 5. Receive the Pattern and the Law 32
  - Step 6. Bringing the Anointing to the People 35
  - Step 7. Dividing the Land 38
  - Ready to Leave Home? 40
- Chapter 03 – Dealing With Pharaoh 44
  - The Pharaoh You Know 45
  - Discontentment Sets In 49
  - Wilderness Wanderings Begin 50
  - Letting Go – No Turning Back 53

- Chapter 04 – Wilderness Wanderings 56
  - The Process Begins 56
  - Time of Growth 63
  - Changing the Pictures 69
  - The Call 71
- Chapter 05 – The Burning Bush Experience 74
  - Confronting Pharaoh Within 75
  - Fearful Thoughts 78
  - God's Representative 81
  - Someone to Lean On 85
  - Enter... Aaron 86
  - Moses Makes the Transition 89
  - The Victor 90
- Chapter 06 – Confronting Pharaoh 94
  - Enter... Joshua 94
  - See it 95
  - Faith Required 96
  - The Answer to People's Prayers 97
  - The Price of the Call 100
- Chapter 07 – Climbing the Mountain 104
  - How You Receive the Mountain Call 104
  - Why You Receive the Mountain Call 109
- Chapter 08 – Receiving The Pattern 118
  - The Progression 118
  - Change Begins With you 122
  - Qualifying for the Next Stage 124

Your Place 126
Chapter 09 – Imparting the Fire 130
    Spread the Fire 130
    Starting a Revival 133
    Prayer 135
Chapter 10 – The 7 Mountain Top Experiences 138
    His Chosen Vessel 141
    Reflecting His Glory 141
    The 1st Visit: The Promise 142
    The 2nd Visit: Making a Contract With God 145
    The 3rd Visit: Confirmation of Your Call 147
Chapter 11 – 4th Visit: Your Ten Commandments 152
    The 4th Visit: The Ten Commandments 155
    The 5th Visit: Impartation 161
Chapter 12 – 6th Visit: The Tabernacle 168
    The Full Picture 169
    The 7th Visit: The Manifest Power of God 172
    A Call to Climb – A Prophetic Decree 180
Chapter 13 – Handling a Rebellious Generation 184
    Change Starts With You 184
    People Are Still Stiff-Necked 185
    Hearts Must Be Ready to Receive 187
    1st Step: Exposing the System 189
    2nd Step: Give Them a Vision 192
    Offer Something Better 194
Chapter 14 – The Slavery Mentality 198

    Remove the Idols 202

Chapter 15 – The New Generation 212

    Signs and Wonders 214

    Fresh Revelation 216

Chapter 16 – Boot Camp: How Moses is Trained 220

    Leadership Training Begins 221

    Intense Preparation for a Greater Ministry 221

    Suddenly Visible 223

    Failure Through Disobedience 224

    Leadership Training 227

    Learning to Let Go 229

    The Uprising From Within 232

    Rejection From Inner Circle 234

    Visible Attack 237

    Aaron's Rod 240

Chapter 17 – The Final Reward 244

    God's Gift to Moses 244

    Driving the Vision Forward 246

    Setting the Structure in Place 246

    Resurrection Time 249

    Hand it Over 250

    Summary 251

Chapter 18 – Birth, Maturation, Death and Resurrection 254

    Make it Real 254

    A Continual Process 256

    The Birth – The Burning Bush 257

The Maturation: Commandments and Precepts	261
Chapter 19 – Handing Over to Joshua	**274**
Death: Returned to the Wilderness	274
Time to Hand Over	276
Resurrection: Taking the Promised Land	280
A Continual Cycle	281
About the Author	**283**
Recommendations by the Author	**284**
The Apostolic Mandate	284
The Apostolic Handbook	284
Driving Your Vision Forward (MP3)	285
How to Get People to Follow You	285
Mentorship 101	286
The Minister's Handbook	286
Pastor Teacher School	287
Contact Information	**288**

CHAPTER 01

DEFINING MOSES

Chapter 01 — Defining Moses

In this new move, we have seen the Lord not only raise up the prophets, but the apostles as well. With this has come a tremendous confusion of what an apostle is and does.

To gain a full understanding, I am going to take you on a journey through the life of Moses. For those of you who are called to be a Moses apostle, you will be astounded to discover that, thousands of years ago, this story, this journey, was penned for you.

God, in His wisdom, has been preparing for this day since the moment that Adam and Eve were settled into the Garden of Eden. He foresaw this very day in which we stand.

It is no mistake that you have travelled the journey that you have, and that you have walked down the wrong and right roads that you have. It is no mistake that you sit here today.

As you have submitted your life to the Lord and have given Him your all, He has ordered your steps to this point in your life. What you do with the outcome of those steps, rests on you.

I pray that in this book, I do not inspire you. I pray that I challenge you and ignite the fire in you to do, not what is right or comfortable, but what God put you on this earth to do. He wants you to establish a pattern in His Church so that it might rise up in glory. He wants you to make a city on a hill that all the nations may look up to.

You and I stand in an era - a magnificent era. We have indeed seen, and will see things, that our forefathers wish they could have seen. There have been intercessors that have travailed in prayer for generation after generation. We are now walking out the fruit of those prayers.

Now, I ask you, what are we doing with the fruit that has been given to this generation? Are we ready, church of God, to build?

The pattern has been given, the plan has been set, and the call has gone out. Even the anointing and power has come. It is time to build the Church.

> **Hebrews 3:1** *Therefore, holy brethren, partakers of the heavenly calling, consider the Apostle and High Priest of our confession, Christ Jesus,*
>
> *2 who was faithful to Him who appointed Him, as Moses also was faithful in all His house.*
>
> *3 For this One has been counted worthy of more glory than Moses, inasmuch as He who built the house has more honor than the house.*

Moses is a picture of an apostolic type. I could have just taken the whole book of Hebrews and slapped it in here, but I did not want to bore you. Here, the writer of Hebrews is comparing the apostle of our faith to Moses.

As I begin to go through Moses' journey, those who are called to this apostolic type are going to have your questions answered. You are going to understand why your journey has been the way that it has.

It is time, apostles, to come forth from the wilderness. It has been a long journey. You have the fire and passion. You have gotten kicked out of Egypt, then ran away and got lost. You have gone into the wilderness, and you have wondered when your time would come.

Consider this the call. It is time to come out of the wilderness. Your time of training is over. It is time to set God's people free now!

How long have you travailed in prayer? How long have you travailed, looking at the church system and written a long list of everything that is wrong?

I can talk to any apostle, and they will have a long list of everything that is wrong in the Church.

So I challenge you with, "What have you done about it?"

> *God holds you accountable. You are the one that He gave the vision to. You are the one that He gave the call to.*

Who was accountable to bring the children of Israel back to the Promised Land?

It was the one who had the encounter with the Lord and had the burning bush experience.

He has given you eyes to see and ears to hear. You have not fully perceived it all, but yet you see what no one else sees. When are you going to build and stop complaining about how the building, at the present time, is built so incorrectly?

DEFINITION OF THE WORD – MANDATE

It is time to fully realize your mandate as an apostle.

So, what is a mandate?

> **Romans 1:1** *Paul, a bondservant of Jesus Christ, called to be an apostle, separated to the gospel of God*
>
> *2 which He promised before through His prophets in the Holy Scriptures,*

Dictionary Definition for Mandate:

> Any contract by which a person undertakes to perform services for another.

Strong's Concordance – Apostle:

> 652 apostolos {ap-os'-tol-os}
>
> AV - apostle 78, messenger 2, he that is sent 1; 81
>
> 1) a delegate, messenger, one sent forth with orders
>
> 1a) specifically applied to the twelve apostles of Christ

I want you to notice how much the word "sent" is repeated here.

Does it say that an apostle is one that sits at home and complains about how terrible the state of the Church is? Does it say that he is one that continues in the old pattern, even though he is so dissatisfied with it?

The apostle is one who is sent!

Apostle Paul tells us that he has been called as an apostle and set apart to be sent. He is not being sent just for the sake of being sent either. He was sent with very clear instructions.

Right now, God is raising up His apostles all over the world. He is putting a pattern, a blueprint, on their hearts for His end-times Church. Apostle of God, what will the Church look like if you do not put your piece of the pattern into place?

One person will not be able to establish this huge body of Christ alone. This is not a room set on a hill, but a city set on a hill. When are you going to fully realize your call and stand in the conviction that God has given to you?

So, let us have a good look at who Moses is.

1. CALLED FROM BIRTH

As we look at the life of Moses, he is one who was called from birth.

Here is the thing - he was not just "called from birth," but he was shaped from then also. We all know that we are called from our mother's womb and so forth. Yet, I want you to consider the time into which Moses was called.

He was born in a very difficult time. You would think that would have brought forth the Deliverer in a time that was a bit more convenient. This was a very inconvenient time for Moses' parents.

This was a time when Pharaoh was killing all the newborn babies. So, when Moses came along, it was not a convenient birth or a planned pregnancy. They did not sit down and say, "Let's have for us a deliverer."

It just happened, and the time in which he was born was an uncomfortable one. He was probably a difficult baby. I know I was.

There was nothing comfortable about his calling from the very time that he first took his breath. From the start, even as a newborn baby, he was different.

He did not try to be different or aim to be different. The time that he was born, and the circumstances surrounding his birth, destined him to be different.

So it is with the Moses apostle. You travail with God.

"Why, Lord, did it have to be like that?"

It is because you were meant to be different. The very circumstances that you were born into, and the difficulty that surrounded all of that, was a sign. The travail and the fact that satan tried to snatch you already from birth was a sign.

The pressure and those circumstances set you on a road that led you to this point today. Look around you. Look at your Aaron, your Miriam, and the rest of your family.

Do they stand where you do today? Why not?

It is because, from the very beginning, God had a plan. He destined you to be out of the ordinary.

2. Sent on a Different Journey (Grew up in Pharaoh's Household)

So yes, Moses was sent on a very different journey.

> *Acts 7:22 And Moses was learned in all the wisdom of the Egyptians, and was mighty in words and deeds.*

This does not make a lot of sense for somebody who is supposed to be the deliverer. You would think that he would have been steeped in his own culture. You would have thought that the Lord would have kept him with his own.

Instead, because of the circumstances into which he was born, his path went so differently to everyone else around him. He ended up learning the things of the world and becoming a prince of Egypt.

It seems so contradictory. When you think about going into the work of the ministry, the last thing that you imagine is that you have to gain the wisdom of the world. Yet, God had a plan.

The Lord needed Moses to think differently to all the slaves of Israel. He had to have a different mentality. So, God arranged the circumstances that, from the very beginning, before he even knew who he was, his mind was already being shaped by the hand of God.

God was using the tools of the world to shape his thinking and to snatch the way that everyone else thought out of him.

The fire and call was always there on your life. Yet, for some strange reason, God did not allow you to go to Bible school like everybody else. When you did, it added nothing to you.

You had to go somewhere else to get what you really felt that you needed. He did not allow you to follow the typical road that everybody else followed. He sent you to Egypt.

"Seriously, Lord? Egypt?"

"Great, you send me to the workplace? You call me and tell me to do marketing? You call me and send me to do all these other things that have nothing to do with You?"

Exactly! Hello, Moses. Your thinking could not be limited to a single vision, calling, and people. Moses saved a lot more than just the Israelites when he left Egypt. There was a lot more that God needed him to accomplish along this journey.

Moses did something that God has also done in you. God has stretched you between two worlds. Moses was put in a situation where he had two sets of parents.

I can imagine how difficult it must have been for him growing up. He was not an Israelite, but he was not an Egyptian. He needed so desperately the affection of a father and a mother.

Yet somehow, just by falling through the cracks and by plain circumstance, he did not get that love and affection that he needed. He was stretched and pushed. There was nothing normal about any of the steps that he took.

When the Lord takes you through those paces, you think, "Lord, why can't I just be like everyone else? Why can't I just be in business or in the Church? Why can't you just make up your mind? Where do you want me?"

"Just when I am here, you send me there. Then, when I am there, you send me here. What is up with that?"

Hello, Moses. The Lord has been shaping you with His very hand.

I am so amazed at how, when God puts a call on your life, He takes care of it. You just need to keep stepping. He is the one that shapes you, brings the circumstances, and puts you into the right home.

> *God is the one that puts you into the right country, job, and circle of friends to shape your mind.*

Our mind is the biggest blockage. Our hearts are open before God, but how we express what is in our hearts comes through our heads. That is where we fall down.

God needed to stretch Moses. He could not think like an Egyptian, and he could not think like an Israelite. He had to have a broader view. Why? Well, let's look further along the way to see what he had to accomplish.

He could not have just a single focus. He had to focus on so many different things. Before he could even begin his journey, he had to be stretched.

3. A Passion to do Things Right (Although not Always in Wisdom)

God put a special heart in Moses. He put a passion in him to do things right. The Moses apostle does not know why, but they just want to do things right.

There is a character forged in them to want to protect and to deliver. They want to reach out and look at the one little slave that is being beaten down by the Egyptian. They want to save that slave and lift him up.

Unfortunately, Moses did not always get it right. He did it in the flesh and killed the Egyptian.

You finally get a conviction of your call, and you are passionate.

"The Lord has called me to reach out and pull out those that are being oppressed and pushed down. I am going to lead them to the Promised Land. I am going to show them how to do it. I am going to raise them up and make them conquerors."

You do it all in the flesh, and then you wonder why you are running from Pharaoh into the wilderness.

There is nothing wrong with the fire of God that you have. However, the way that you walked it out was with all of your natural ability. Then, you hit a wall, good and solid.

That is the next phase of coming to understand that it is not by might, nor by power, but by His spirit. That is how you are going to accomplish this call.

So, Moses hit the wall, and he saw that he was not the big deliverer that he thought he was. He was not the "hot shot" that was going to lead the people out of Egypt.

Then, you sit there thinking, "Lord, why did you give me all these visions if I cannot fulfill them? Why did you give me all these plans? Why did you give me eyes to see, just for me to reach out and try to bring change, only for someone to try to kill me?

I do not get it. Why would you give me all of this stuff and then not allow me to walk it out? When I try to walk it out, I mess it up."

4. Learning to Serve

He needed to learn to serve. Moses finally got a conviction of his call and realized that God had something amazing for his life. Then, he got called to serve another man.

Moses found himself in the wilderness, having to submit to his father-in-law, Jethro. Did he remain there for four days, four weeks, or four years?

Forty years!

Perhaps he was a slow learner. You think that you have it bad! God would not release Moses until he had truly learned to serve. He needed to serve as a son would serve. He served as a shepherd and was always serving another man's vision.

From Servant to Leader

Now personally, submission was a bit of a problem for me because, "I hear God better…" right?!

"Why should I submit to that unrighteousness?"

When I learned to submit and serve, and not begrudgingly, I gained a servant's heart. I learned what it is to be a servant. I thought like a servant, I walked like a servant, and I talked like a servant. I became a vessel of servanthood.

Once I had fully become that vessel and was comfortable there, God said, "It is over. Now, it is time to set my people free."

Now, I was on the other side of the coin. I had to learn to be a leader. I was very much like Moses, travailing with God, "I cannot speak like that. I am not a 'hot shot'. When I do open my mouth, I upset people.

I am happy in servanthood. I am happy making someone else look good. That way, if there is a mistake, they can take the blame. If anything goes wrong, they will take the fall."

So, the Lord switched it around, and suddenly, I was the one in charge. It was a terrifying place to be. I was not a servant or a follower anymore. I had to learn to become a leader.

I was stretched. I had been a servant, a spiritual daughter, and a disciple. So when I became the leader and mentor, I had the full picture. I could look at them and say, "I know exactly what you are thinking right now."

Since I had been in their shoes, I could also say, "This is how you need to deal with it."

Can you not see that God has already been giving you pieces of a blueprint? He was not calling you to serve just to prove a lesson to you. He was not trying to put you down or chisel you. He was trying to give you a piece of the pattern.

> **It is only when you learn to serve that you truly understand how to lead.**

You can look and see every single person and say, "I know your place."

The reason why you know this is because you have been in every one of those places.

From there you can say, "I have a pattern and a picture for you. This is how we are going to do it."

You can take the revelation that God gives you and as a leader say, "I know how that feels. This is going to happen, and that person is going to come against you. Let's make a plan."

You have been there. It was not wasted time with Jethro. God was using it, not for Jethro's sake, but for your own.

5. Waiting on God's People to Become Ready

Have you ever asked God the question, "When will you release me?"

God will release you when His people are ready. He has been preparing you for this moment in time, but there is a little bit more to it than what you think.

The Scriptures tell us that when the Israelites began to cry out, God sent them Moses as their deliverer.

Moses, why have you been waiting so long?

Did you fail God?

Is it because you messed up and were not strong enough as a leader?

Is it because you did not say it or do it right?

Did you miss the call and make some bad choices?

Have you made too many mistakes?

None of the above. God's people have not been ready for your pattern then - but now they are.

You have gotten so comfortable under Jethro and in the wilderness. Now, God has to send you a burning bush to get you to move.

Moses changed! He was so ready to save the world, kill the Egyptian, and set God's people free. However, the very people he was trying to change turned their backs on him.

The very people that you were trying to help say, "Who do you think you are? Who are you, coming with all your revelations and big ideas? You need to settle down."

They tattled behind your back to Pharaoh, getting you into trouble and tearing you down from behind.

All you were trying to do was the work of God. You were just trying to fulfill the call on your life. Yet, you were chased out of Egypt.

This is running through your mind as you are taking care of all that goat poop.

You think, "I am on the poop parade because I missed God. I missed my time of visitation. I was not obedient at the right time, so the mantle has passed by me."

Moses, it has not even begun. That was just preparation. God was just positioning you, waiting for his people to be ready. He put you in the right place, at the right time, for the right people. He did this in order for you to fulfill your purpose. Can't you see that?

> *You have not been waiting on God, but on His people's hearts to be ready for the message that you have.*

I am here to say, "God's people are ready!"

The evangelists have gone forth and brought down the fire. The teachers have gone in with the Word and started to break up the stony hearts. However, they need a pattern to build by.

Otherwise, we are just going to have a fivefold ministry that is scattered throughout the Church. It will be like fingers running around independently. Creepy.

It is the apostle that needs to bring the hand together. Then, we can function as a team and fulfill our purpose.

We have seen all of the fivefold ministry take their turn to shine. This is what we have been experiencing for the last ten to fifteen years. We have already experienced the prophetic move.

Now it is time for you, Moses, to begin to build. We need to bring each of these movements into focus and give them a structure where they can function correctly.

6. Multi-faceted Calling

Can you understand now why you had to go into so many different departments?

"What am I, Lord? Am I an evangelist, a teacher, a pastor, or a prophet?"

You are an apostle.

"What is the core of what you are called to do?"

"I guess I can win someone for the Lord, teach if I need to teach, prophesy if I need to prophesy. The Lord has sent me on such a journey that I think I am destined to wander around in the wilderness. I will never know what I am doing. I will just give a word here and a healing there."

It is time to bring it together. It is time for you to realize that each one of these experiences has forged something in you. With each experience, you have been as Moses, receiving a piece of the pattern.

I can imagine, when they started to build the tabernacle, it looked a little strange. There was a pole over here, some badger skin there, and a Cherubim there. It was all disconnected.

This has been your experience so far. God has sent you here and there. Just when you get it, He pulls you back.

"I thought this was my calling."

"It was, but hold on that."

Then, He sends you somewhere else.

"I am fulfilling my calling now!"

"Come back."

"I thought that this was my calling?"

"It was, but now I need you to go here."

You are thinking, "Which one is my calling? They are so diverse."

"I am a trainer, a pastor, a father, and I am cleaning toilets. Lord, can you just focus, please?"

He is trying to bring focus, just give Him time. Each one of these roads that He sends you down are forging something different in you. Sometimes, they are even completely opposite to anything that you know.

You are thinking, "I am really off my rocker. That is so different to anything that I have done before."

Good, that was obviously the missing piece that you needed. It is time now to start fulfilling your mandate. This will require pulling from each one of those experiences and callings.

That is why, when you look at the apostolic calling, you are not going to see just one call. You are going to see a collection of callings. It will be neatly arranged into a structured organization that is meant to mature, instruct, and raise up the body of Christ.

You cannot do that with just one call.

> **You cannot set a pattern in place for the Church just with evangelism and a prophetic word.**

You cannot do it with one revelation from the Word, or even just as a spiritual parent. You need them all.

Chapter 02

The Moses Apostle

Chapter 02 – The Moses Apostle

There is a lot that goes on in a city. There are streets, traffic lights, plumbing, electricity, and so forth. There is a lot to be done in a city. We are called to build a city on a hill, not one little room or one little house – a city!

That is why the Lord has sent you on so many different roads. He has been weaving quite the picture for you, hasn't He? He sent out all of the other fivefold ministries. Even you have operated in those different fivefold ministries, to prepare the hearts of God's people.

Perhaps God told you a long time ago that you have an apostolic call?

You said, "Yes!" Then, he told you to go and be an evangelist.

God called you to be an apostle, and the next thing you know, you have to be a pastor. You have to be nice to people and travail long with them.

He was doing two things. On one hand, He was preparing the Church for the apostolic move. On the other hand, He was preparing you for the apostolic move because it is up to you to bring it all together.

So, let us look at what happened when it was time for Moses to finally begin his journey.

Step 1. Confronting Pharaoh

"Yes, I am called to be an apostle and to go out there and lead God's people back. I have been through all of these phases and the preparation. God has given me the go ahead. He told me to step out in faith."

The first thing you are going to confront is Pharaoh - the world system. Finances! How are you going to take care of your finances?

Where are you going to start this work? Where are you going to get your team from?

Oppositions are going to start coming from all sides. At first, because you face that opposition, you think, "Did I hear from God?"

God says to Moses, "Go back and set my people free."

He gave him miracles. Moses had snakes and leprosy to prove his point – he had a whole party going on there. I can imagine after Aaron met Moses in the wilderness, no further confirmation was needed.

He thought, "We are going to go in there, march up to Pharaoh, and he is going to let God's people go. Then, we are going to dance out of here."

What was the first thing that he faced?

It was a big, fat door in his face.

"I guess it is not of God. If it is God's plan, He will make a way. If it is His will, it is His bill."

"The door did not open. I just experienced warfare and opposition. People did not understand. My finances did not immediately start coming right, and things did not happen. I must have missed God."

Are you really going to give up in the first step, Moses? Are you so easily deterred after all that you have been through?

For goodness sakes, look at your journey. Are you going to let a little bit of Pharaoh get you down?

Are you going to throw in the towel because someone that is "high and mighty" tells you, "No?"

> *The first thing that you are going to face is a higher level of spiritual warfare than you have ever faced before.*

Why is that?

Do you really think that satan is just going to let God's people go with a dance and a song? You have to fight for it.

He has had them in bondage for this long. Did you think that the first time you preached your message that everyone would open their hearts and say, "Please come and revolutionize our church?"

"Please come and change the way that I have thought for fifty years. I am dying for you to tell me that I have done it wrong all this time."

You are going to get opposition. However, God still has a plan. Even though Moses faced opposition again and again - with miracle after miracle, God vindicated him. That will be the proof of your journey.

It is not the great, big, open doors, or the sudden invitations to come and preach. The fact is, no matter what anyone says against you or does to you, God will always vindicate you.

He will vindicate you because you are His chosen vessel.

You have been in the palm of His hand from the time you took your first breath. He has carried you to this point. Did you think that He would forsake you now?

Did you think that He would carry you this far and make you walk the rest of the way?

No, He is here to continue to carry you and make sure that you fulfill this purpose that He has on your life.

STEP 2. SET THE CAPTIVES FREE

The next step of his journey was to set the captives free. Here we see a very strong evangelistic orientation. I do not care if you are called to be an apostle. You better get used to the fact that you are going to experience all of the fivefold ministry.

I discussed the progress of this in the *Called to the Ministry* book, so I am not going to labor on it here. God is going to take you through all of the fivefold ministry so that you can understand and bring them together.

He will have you be prophetic, and then the next thing you know, you will be working with the lost. He will have you go out and do things that have nothing to do with your ministry vision.

How else did you think that you were going to set the captives free? Again, there is confrontation. There is confrontation with demons - warfare within and warfare without. Warfare within your home, warfare without your home. Pressure, pressure, pressure.

Keep stepping because God is not done with you yet. Moses, this is your journey. Your journey is shaping you to lay a foundation for this end-times Church.

STEP 3. TO TRAIN AND EQUIP

Then, God is going to have you train and equip. The children of Israel were in captivity for years. We are not looking at a well-structured army here.

When they faced their first battle, who do you think taught them to fight? Do you think that it was any mistake that God sent Moses into the courts of Pharaoh to learn all of those secrets? Those secrets would have included warfare for that day and age.

Suddenly, why God sent you in all those directions starts to make sense. You need to train and equip God's people.

Just when you are so excited about being an evangelist, God changes it up and has you start training, equipping, and raising up the leaders. You have to get them into formation and get them to be battle ready.

Then, He has you raise up the leaders. Jethro pays Moses a visit and says, "What are you doing, Moses? You are killing yourself."

Moses still had a bit of status quo in him at this point. He thought he had to be the senior pastor and the only one that could answer everybody's questions.

His father comes along and says, "You are going to kill yourself, man. You need to give yourself a break. You need to set up leaders of ten, hundreds, and thousands. You need to take the anointing that is on you and pass it down to them."

STEP 4. RAISE UP LEADERS

The Moses apostle is not one who keeps the anointing to himself. The Moses apostle is one that has this revolutionary idea and says, "I want to raise up other leaders like myself, or higher than myself."

I want to take everything that God has given to me, and I want to invest it into them so that they can go out and change the world.

"What is wrong with you?"

You are just a Moses. That heart burns in you. You are not content to be the senior pastor or the only leader out there. You have a heart to raise up other leaders, and to send them out.

That is why your journey has been so long because God is going to send you leaders of tens, hundreds, and thousands. Every single one of them are going to be different. You better have enough of a pattern to be able to give something to each one of those leaders.

Then, they will be able to rise up in the realm that God has called them to.

That is why you had to do it all. Those leaders that come to you are going to be very specific. Each of those leaders were in charge of a little tribe and family. Their calling was quite focused.

Yet, let's look at Moses. His calling was so diverse, and yours is too.

It needs to be so that, when God brings you all of these leaders, you can say, "This is your division. You are evangelistic. Your place is here. Let me give you that anointing that God has given me. You can come and sit under me because I have gone through that, and you need it."

"You are prophetic. You have a call to set the captives free and to bring forth inner healing. I know that. I know where you belong. Come here, and let me put you in charge of your tens, hundreds, and thousands."

So, we see Moses as a coordinator, one who brings all the pieces together. Why does he qualify? It is because he walked all those roads. That is why this calling is not one that comes lightly, or one that comes to the young.

The Moses apostles that we have worked with are on in years. Why is this? It is because there was a whole lot of living to do. I do not think that you can truly appreciate it, until you have walked that road yourself and travailed long, again and again.

You will only see the fruit of that travail when God brings you those leaders, and you suddenly have the answer. You do not try to have the answer, but to you, it is obvious.

People say, "How do you get that wisdom?"

You think, "I have been around the block a few times… you should meet my goats."

"You have no idea the roads that I have walked to get here. I did that just so that I might impart to you this one thing that will help you fulfill your call."

Hello, Moses. Is your journey beginning to make sense? It is glorious, isn't it?

Oh yeah! Sign me up for apostle now. I want to die daily. I want to live and make all the mistakes for everyone else. I want to be the scum of the earth. I want to be left behind while everyone else rises up.

I want to sit on the mountain, gazing at the Promised Land thinking, "I would love to have one of those peaches, but I cannot."

Do you still think that this is a glorious calling?

When all is said and done, you are going to sit on your mountaintop and die.

However, your reward will be in the fact that the land is taken. We will have left behind an inheritance that will continue from generation to generation.

So, before you think that the call to apostleship is one of glory, let me bring you down a few notches. You have no idea of the price.

I know one that is ready to be an apostle. He is one that has been so humbled by God and paid such a price, serving and travailing, that he does not count himself worthy and does not even recognize the treasure that God has put in him.

He does not recognize that treasure until such a time when God brings him the leaders of tens, hundreds, and thousands. Suddenly, a well is opened up, and all that anointing that God invested into him, year after year, comes flooding out.

He thinks, "Whoa! Where did that come from?"

It was all stored up behind a dam.

STEP 5. RECEIVE THE PATTERN AND THE LAW

Moses has to receive the pattern and the law. That is very much part of the journey. Much of the training that the Moses apostle goes through is a training on the run. There is no time to sit and be complacent.

The only time that he got to rest was when he died. So, do not look forward to the rest too quickly. We would like to keep you for a little while longer on this earth.

There was always something else going on. He had to go up the mountain again and again to receive the pattern and the law.

What did he do with that pattern?

He came down, and he gave it to the people. For his great reward, he did not even get to enter into the secret place. Aaron did.

I like being Aaron because you get to go into the Holy of Holies. I love being Joshua because you can linger long, pick up your sword, and take on the enemy. You also get to break ground, take the land, and get out there. However, one day the Lord said to me, "You are Moses. Go and stand on the hill."

"But Joshua is down there, and look, he is having so much fun. Can I just join Joshua?"

"Sit on the hill, Moses."

"Fine," I said with my hands lifted up.

Everyone else gets to have all the fun. You travail long, die, and resurrect. You give up, get stripped and taken from, and people take advantage of you. You fulfill another man's vision, just to stand on a hill and have someone else walk in your anointing.

Are you sure that you still want to walk out this apostolic call? Are you sure that you want to pay this price?

The price of the apostolic is not giving up your car, house, family and countries. You haven't even begun. The greatest price is discovered when you get there. You discover it when you are standing on the hill, and Joshua gets to have all the fun.

All you get to have is a sore back and arms from holding up your stick saying, "Go Joshua! Go Joshua!"

That nearly killed me. If there was ever a price for me in this calling, it was that. I am the boots-on-the-ground, sword-in-hand, type of person. I want to have ten swords and go and take down the enemy.

God says to me, "Get comfortable up there, Moses."

You will see everyone rising up, taking ground, and getting in there.

I am like, "Kill me now. This is what I went through for? Just for this?"

However, because of what Moses went through, there was an anointing that rested on him. In travail, he birthed a pattern and anointing. Since he had that, the Lord could bring him all those leaders, and he could stand.

Because he stood, the war was won.

It is a strange transition. You are so used to doing, doing, doing, and being the trailblazer. Yet, you need to stand back, allow the anointing that is on you to go on others, and watch them take the land.

It is indeed the fulfillment of the call on your life. Are you beginning to get a picture of your mandate, apostle?

You are not only going to establish a pattern, but you are going to bring together all the pieces and raise up those leaders.

> *When all is said and done, you will have given up your personal time, finances, and your very life for each one. Then, you will step back and let them walk in your anointing and look glorious in your stead.*

That is how we are going to change the Church. One man cannot change the Church. We need the anointing and the pattern. We also need the men and women who are willing to stay on the mountain in that pattern and anointing.

We need them to stand in faith, and with confidence, and say, "You go there, you go there, and you go there. I am covering you."

That is the price that the Moses apostle is called to pay.

Step 6. Bringing the Anointing to the People

He is not one who keeps all the anointing to himself. He went up the mountain, and he had a face-to-face encounter with the Father. When he came down, he brought the glory with him.

I will teach more about this process in later chapters, how Moses took the elders and Joshua up. The point was that he did not keep the glory for himself. He brought the glory down for the people, that they might touch God.

Apostle Paul said, "You are the fruit of our labor. We work, we sow, and you eat and get fat. We are skinny. You are fat. We are poor. You are rich."

Do you still want to be an apostle? Do you still think it is such a glorious position?

What an investment. Paul sat in prison, writing his letters, hungry and alone. It was to the point where some of those close to him started to doubt him. He said, "Are you going to forsake me too?"

Yet today, you and I are the fruit of his mandate. Five, ten, or fifty years down the line, who will be the fruit of the mandate that God has put in your life?

Would you rather have the present glory?

Do you want to taste the good fruit now and be glorified now? Well – you have your reward. You are famous, and people think that you are fantastic.

You can die now, Moses. Your job is done. In fact, please move aside.

I do not want to leave that kind of heritage behind.

"She lived. She was glorious. She died."

I would like to remain in each leader that rises up. I want to remain in each Joshua that picks up the sword. I want to remain in each Aaron that enters into the secret place, that we might gather this pattern.

That is the thing about the Moses apostle. God has given you this heart.

When I meet someone who says that they have an apostolic call, you must know that I am looking at you, and I am looking for this heart. I am looking for a heart to give, to raise up others, and to put others in your place.

I am looking to see that you will decrease so that they may increase. That is the heart of a Moses. If we raise up these leaders in the Church today, we will have a city on a hill. We are going to have a glorious Church where every believer can touch God.

They will be able to experience power in every part of their lives. That is the vision. What is your mandate in that vision, apostle? Have you started bringing the pieces together, or are you just running around sharing that you are called to be an apostle?

Good for you! What are you doing about it?

I am glad that you are called to be an apostle. That is fantastic. Show me your fruit. Show me your pattern.

Are you waiting for someone to come and hand it to you because you do not feel like going down all of those uncomfortable roads?

Though, you know that God keeps calling you down those roads, don't you?

"Lord, I am on in years. I have already been through enough training. I do not think that I need to go through anymore."

That is fine. You can stay where you are. You can be comfortable on your plateau. In fact, put up a tent because you are going to be there for a while. You are not moving forward until you finish that process.

I sense that challenge right now. God has a timetable for His Church. He has been training you alongside that timetable because His people have started to cry out.

However, He is not going to release you until you have walked all those roads. Otherwise, you are going to put together a pattern that is incomplete. When Moses got the pattern for the tabernacle, he did not wing it. It was very specific.

The height, the width, the depth, the color, and the design were specific. You are not going to get that kind of clarity if you do not walk down all of the roads that God has called you to walk down.

In the spirit, I see that there is a road that God continues to ask you to walk down, but you keep struggling with it.

"I am an apostle. Why should I walk down that road?"

It is because you are an apostle that you need to walk down that road. Do you not get it?

"I have this high calling. Why should I be on the poop parade?"

It is because you have this high calling that you are called to the poop. That is how it is. That is the very missing piece. You are looking for something up there, and the Lord is saying, "Lower… lower… lower…"

Jesus could do it.

You would think that in order to usher in the revelation of the Son of God, He would have been someone of great renown. There should have been someone that could herald and shout that the Son of God had come.

However, He was born in a stable. Jesus knew poop from a very young age. So, what makes you think that you are any higher than Him?

Our very savior could go down on His knees and serve, traveling on this road and that. He ministered with Nicodemus, hung out with prostitutes, and did some preaching. He spent time with the Father, walked on water, and ministered to His disciples.

There are so many things that He did, so many roads that He went down.

Are you too good for this road and journey because you think that you already have it all together?

If you think that you already have all that and do not need to go down any of those roads, then you are plateauing in your call.

STEP 7. DIVIDING THE LAND

An important part of Moses' journey was dividing the land. He prepared for the generations to come.

Not only did he train up the leaders and set the pattern in place for how we need to do things now, but he always had this foresight. He would sit with Joshua and say, "This is how we are going to divide the land."

Even before he could fully see all of it, he was already making a plan for the future.

"When I am gone, Joshua, this family is going to give you a hard time. You will need to put these guys here, and you will need to take care of this and that problem."

> *Sometimes, we get so wrapped up in our call, our vision, and our "now experience" in the glory that we forget there is a generation to come.*

I daresay that the generation of today in the Church is lacking because the generation of yesterday had no foresight.

If they would have set a pattern in place, would it not be so much easier for all of us to fulfill our calling?

Well, guess what? God just made you accountable. You are accountable for the next generation. If you can leave a pattern behind that they can walk in, you have changed the Church.

You do not just change it for one meeting or one revival. It is good that you experienced so many wonderful things, but what about the next generation?

What foundation have you laid in the hearts of God's people? What structure have you set?

"I do not need structure. I prophesy here and there, and I go here and there and sell my books."

So do millions of other people! I am so happy that you are so proud of yourself. One day, you will die, and your books will no longer be sold and nobody will know your name.

If you are cool with that, then I am cool with that. However, a Moses is not so cool with that.

He wants more than just a prophetic word that is here today and gone tomorrow. The only reason why some remember them is because they scribble them down or record them on their iPhones. Then, they play them back over and over again.

I want to leave way more behind than a prophetic word on someone's iPhone. I would like to think that I have left behind a structure, a pattern and a law. I want to have done this both practically, and in the hearts of God's people.

I do not want the Church to just stay the same, but to progress from glory to glory, even in my absence. Not every apostolic type is called to this, but Moses, you are. You have quite the journey ahead of you.

I hope that I have put the fear of God in you because this is not a call for the lighthearted. Before you get all comfortable with throwing the word "apostle" around, you need to be accountable.

If you tell me that you are an apostle, I am going to ask you this question, "Why is the church of God in the state that it is in, apostle? Please explain to me why you are not doing your job.

Do not dare wear this title until you are doing something about it. Show me the fruit. Show me your pattern, and show me your inheritance. I want to see it."

Ready to Leave Home?

The Church needs to see this from you. The people of God are indeed ready. They are crying out for a deliverer. Are you ready to leave your comfort zone behind? Are you ready to leave home?

Are you ready to leave your spiritual dad, if that is what God is calling you to do? The person that you have been serving under, the place that you have been in - are you ready to step away and answer the call?

The minute that you do, the anointing will increase. The apostolic anointing will increase.

> *The apostolic anointing is a weighty anointing because it is one that comes directly from the throne of the Father.*

It is not like the prophet, who draws you into an embrace and a relationship with Jesus, telling you that everything is alright.

It is an experience with the Father that shows you everything that is wrong. It shows you everything that needs to be changed, renovated, built, and equipped.

It is a weighty call and a heavy anointing. Yes, you are going to need your Aaron and Hur to hold up your arms. It is going to get heavy. The spiritual warfare is heavy because you are not fighting just for your ministry and your church.

You are fighting for the church of God. You are fighting on behalf of the King of Kings, and that is a weighty responsibility.

You will stand on top of the mountain and see Joshua with the sword in his hand. You will think, "He does this so well."

You will know that you are the one that put that sword in his hand. You will look over that land and realize what the Lord has used you to do.

"Lord, I have brought your people to the Promised Land. Lord, I look back over my life, and I see that I have snatched your mighty warriors from the hand of satan. I am leading them, showing them, and leaving something behind."

That is the reward. It is only a Moses apostle that even considers that a reward and the joy of the call.

THERE IS NO "FINAL DESTINATION"

There is no final destination for the Moses apostle. There is only the journey. Just when you think that you are "all that" and have the piece of the pattern that you need, your journey will take yet another step.

That is probably why I revel in it so much. There is always a new level to go to. There are always more captives to set free and more leaders that need to be trained.

There are always more leaders that need a place and need the anointing. There is always a greater structure and a greater building that needs to be built.

> **Your training and experience is in the journey.**

Stop looking for the final destination and realize that your tomorrow is now.

The day in which you stand right now is your destination. Every step you take is your destination. You are building and establishing with every single step.

It is time to take that step and to make yourself accountable for the call and the condition of the Church.

Daniel was a very righteous man, but yet he wept and travailed for the sins of his forefathers. He made himself accountable for sins that he never committed.

Jesus travailed in the Garden of Gethsemane and was taken to the cross. He travailed for sins that He never committed. God calls to you saying, "Apostle, are you ready to travail and make yourself accountable for the condition of the Church?

Are you ready to put your money where your mouth is? Are you ready to take what you see and hear and do something about it? Are you ready to set my people free?"

CHAPTER 03

DEALING WITH PHARAOH

Chapter 03 – Dealing With Pharaoh

Psalms 77:16-20:

> *The waters saw you, O God, the waters saw you; they were afraid: the depths also were troubled.*
>
> *17 The clouds poured out water: the skies sent out a sound: your arrows also went abroad.*
>
> *18 The voice of your thunder [was] in the heaven: the lightnings lightened the world: the earth trembled and shook.*
>
> *19 Your way [is] in the sea, and your path in the great waters, and your footsteps are not known.*
>
> *20 You led your people like a flock by the hand of Moses and Aaron.*

As you read this Scripture, did you get a picture of how magnificent our God is? How awesome, how huge, and how He is beyond anything our minds can comprehend? See how His ways are not known and how His footsteps are in the ocean.

Look at your magnificent God.

This is the God that the Moses apostle knows.

This is the God that the Moses apostle speaks to face-to-face. It is this God that the Moses apostle introduces God's people to, and before you can even begin on this path called apostolic training, you must come face-to-face with this God.

In this chapter, I am going to take you on a journey - from where you were to where you should be. I'm going to take you on a journey from apostolic nothing, to apostolic preparation, to training. I'm going to take you from where you were not even called to where you should be going.

Perhaps you have walked this path already, and you will be able to identify this journey. Perhaps you are busy walking this road. Perhaps you have not yet walked this road. So, as you read, see where along this journey you are, because each apostle is traveling this road, but at a different pace.

Some have gone before us, and some will come behind us. If you are called to be an apostle, sooner or later you are going to walk this road. Sooner or later, you will see the landmarks and the signs that say, "Oh yes, I know where I am now!"

Perhaps with the grace and the anointing of the Holy Spirit, I can help point out some of these landmarks to you. I can help say, "This is where you are in your journey. This is what to expect. This is why you faced what you did on your journey."

A New Foundation

And so, I invite you to walk this road with me. It is a road set in the time of Moses, before any of the Law, or any of what we know as structure even was. They had no Law or anything to go on. They didn't know who this God was, or even how man originated.

There was nothing! It was a clean slate. Then came Moses who introduced a pattern and a foundation for the whole of the nation of Israel, and even for the Church today. Today, as we stand and look ahead of us at the end-times Church and what is to come, we stand, once again, with a clean slate before us.

There is still much to be written and much to be done. There is much that needs to be completed. Just as Moses went ahead with the children of Israel, prepared the way, and laid the foundation, so you are even now being called to the end-times Church, to go ahead and lay a foundation.

So, follow the life of Moses with me, and let's have a look and see where it all began.

The Pharaoh You Know

Moses was born into the courts of Pharaoh. What is Pharaoh? This one should not be very difficult for you. If you have read my book

The Key of David when I said, "What is Saul?" the answer was easy. Saul represents the system.

It is the same thing for Pharaoh. Pharaoh represents the system - but not just any system. He represents the world system. You see, Saul represented the Church system, but Pharaoh represents more than that. He represents the world and the Church - the world in the Church!

To become a Moses apostle, Pharaoh needs to be separated from you.

Pharaoh has been bred into you. He has been bred into the way you view ministry and the way you operate in it, in the way you see the Church.

That has to be separated from who and what you are, before you can rise up in this mandate. Before you can meet this Almighty God that I have shared about, you must remove every template, every mindset, and every archetype that prevents you from coming face-to-face with God the Father.

Until all those veils have been removed, you cannot meet God. Until all those things that are coloring your view and blinding you from the truth have been removed, you cannot rise up to be the apostle that He has called you to be.

With that being said, you will see and understand why you have had to face the preparation that you have faced.

It says in Acts 7:22:

> *And Moses was learned in all the wisdom of the Egyptians, and was mighty in words and in deeds.*

Challenging The Pharaoh In You

He was born into the house of Pharaoh. Moses did not have a choice here. He couldn't say where he was going to be born or what he was going to do.

It is very likely that the Moses apostle grew up in a Christian home. He has known "religion" all his life. It is something that he has always done and is familiar with. Many churchy and religious templates have been built into you during your entire lifetime.

How do I know this? I am one of them. I was born into a Christian home and had about three or four generations of Christians on either side.

You grow up just knowing, "This is how things are and how they are done. This is the way things operate around here. This is church. Church means you wake up on a Sunday morning and say, 'Oh mom, do we have to wake up so early?'"

Mom says, "Yes, hurry up! Get dressed. We're late."

You get in the car, and you make it there just in time. Then, you sit down and time the sermon and how long the pastor takes to finish that prayer! Then, you get up, and you go home.

That was church for me as a young child. It was never anything exciting! It was just what you did. You got up, you went to church, you fellowshipped a bit, and then you went home.

You grew up in it, and you didn't think, "It shouldn't be any different."

That was just the way things were, and all those templates were built into you that said, "This is the way things are done."

YOU GROW UP

Then, you grow up. Moses grew up, and what happened? He joined the court. He learned their law and how they operated. He became strong in his words and deeds within the court of Pharaoh. Why shouldn't he? That's all he knew!

He was born into the court. He naturally grew up in the court and became somebody of renown in it. Is that not the way the natural order of things goes?

Hey, I was a pastor's kid. These things were expected of me. I was born in the church, so naturally I should grow up in the church. By the time I was thirteen years old, I was in the worship band. At the age of fourteen, I stood up and gave my first sermon. It was just the natural order of things. It is what you did, and it was what was expected of you.

So, further templates were built on what ministry is, and what ministry should be. I never questioned it. It was what had been built into me all my life. Why should I question it? It was the right way of doing things, wasn't it? That is the way the church was run.

WHERE IS THE REALITY?

You know something, I may have grown up in the church, and I may have had the truth. But, it was still not enough. We were Pentecostal, Charismatic, Spirit-filled, Word-based – you name it – we had it sorted.

I went to a Baptist church, and I experienced a Methodist church as well - every kind of denomination you can think of. I knew what God was. I had a foundation in the Word.

You know what I didn't have? I didn't have an experience with God the Father. It was all in my mind. It was all the "knowing how and how-to and the what-ifs." I knew all that stuff. I knew what I was supposed to be. I knew where I was supposed to be going, but it wasn't a reality to me.

It was church. It was religion. It was just the way things were done.

It was a case of, "Well, I suppose that's my lot in life."

There was no reality. Since all of these things and preconceived ideas and mindsets blocked my view, it prevented me from seeing God as He really was. I took Him for granted. He was nothing magnificent. He was just a God that we served on Sundays.

We spoke about God so often that He was "just God." He was just that guy we talked to at prayer meetings and at church all the time. He wasn't a reality.

DISCONTENTMENT SETS IN

It's around this time that you become discontent. You think, "There's got to be something more to church than this!"

You look around, and you see all your friends out in the world. They are having a good time, and you are thinking, "You know what? I'm missing something." You start feeling unsettled.

You say, "Now why is it that they are having so much fun out there in the world, and yet it is so dead in the Church? How come everybody is going into the world to have their needs met, and they are not being met in the Church?"

You start looking around you, and you become restless. You start becoming discontented and dissatisfied.

In your restlessness, you say, "I know this is the way it's always been and the way I've always known it, but something is missing. There has to be something more! There must be something deeper."

That is the apostolic call! If you weren't restless, and if you were complacent just to sit and be that all your life, then you wouldn't have picked this book up in the first place!

You were restless. You kept saying, "There has to be more! There has to be something deeper and greater! I can't stay on this plateau for the rest of my life.

You say, "I hear about all these great revivals of times gone by. Now I look at the Church, and it is just stuck in the system. People are dead! There's no love. There's no unity and no hope. There is nothing!"

Moses looked around. He saw the children of Israel growing up in the courts of Pharaoh, and he became restless.

He looked at them and thought, "It shouldn't be this way! The children of Israel shouldn't be bound. They shouldn't be under the Egyptians. This is wrong. I don't care if this is the way I was brought up! This doesn't fit. It shouldn't be this way. I want freedom for my people."

The final thought sets in that goes beyond discontentment. After looking around at what is wrong, you say… "I want to change it."

Wilderness Wanderings Begin

So Moses did what all of us do. He rose up in his flesh, and he did it his way. He was Mr. Bigmouth, standing up and saying, "This is the way it's going to be done guys. This is wrong. That's wrong. We've got to change this!"

Without the leading of the Holy Spirit, you got in there and started saying, "This is what has to change, and that has to change."

You go to the leader of the ministry you are under and say, "You know, the Lord's given me this pattern, and this is the way we should be running things."

What do you think the first thing that happens is? Pharaoh finds out!

He says, "Moses, you've been on your own agenda there, doing what you want to do. You're messing with my nice, comfortable little structure here, Moses. I don't like it when somebody messes with my structure!"

Escaping the Pressure

So Moses ran out for fear of his life. Is this sounding familiar yet?

I did the same thing. We were helping out in a little local church. My dad, at that time, was the assistant pastor, and I was playing the drums in the worship band. Oh man, they were so legalistic! I just looked at this fallacy, and I wanted to get in there and change things.

So I did what every good Christian girl did. I went and spoke to the pastor's wife, and I started giving counsel to the pastor's son and daughter.

Well, that didn't go too well with the pastor. I started introducing them to concepts and saying, "You know what? There's more to being a Christian than just do's and don'ts. There's life. There's reality. There's more than this!"

I even introduced them to some "way-out" Christian gospel rock music! Needless to say, it was not taken too well. I was messing with the structure.

They said, "This is the way it is. This is the way you dress. This is the way you act. This is the way we have meetings on Sundays, and you don't mess with that."

I did what Moses did. I ran. I put down my drumsticks, and I ran. I stopped playing the drums, and I stopped being interested in the things of God. I just let it all go.

I said, "You know what? I'm not prepared to face this!"

THE GREAT ESCAPE

You know, Moses didn't even face Pharaoh and explain things. He ran. David was kicked out and had to run because Saul was after him, but it was not quite the same thing with Moses.

Moses ran out of fear, and out of rejection. He just couldn't bear to face it. David kept hanging on, and the Lord had to practically kick him out from Saul's court and say, "Hey, get lost!"

> *For Moses, it was different. He left there saying, "I can't face this rejection! I can't face people not liking me. I can't handle this. The pressure is too much for me to handle."*

So, he just dropped everything and backed off. He moved into the background and went off into the wilderness.

Have you been there? I know that's what happened to me.

I said, "I can't take this pressure."

INTO THE WILDERNESS

I said, "I can't take this. This is too much for me. I can't face this kind of rejection and this pressure in my life. I cannot live up to those expectations. I am not like them. I'm different. I cannot think like them, and I don't want to think like them!"

So, instead of standing up, I withdrew, and I went off into the wilderness.

Perhaps that is where you are right now, and you are thinking, "Man, I really missed it! I should have said something. I should have done something. You know, I'm really a second-rate Christian. Nobody probably even knows I'm a Christian because I'm just not even doing anything."

That is the way it is supposed to be, because it is in the wilderness that the Lord is going to start dealing with all those mindsets and templates.

He will deal with all the "churchiness" and the religion in you that is preventing you from entering in. It is being stripped off you one by one and bit by bit.

So, you leave the courts of Pharaoh.

> ***Acts 7:24*** *And seeing one of them suffer wrong, he defended and avenged him who was oppressed, and struck down the Egyptian.*
>
> *25 For he supposed that his brethren would have understood that God would deliver them by his hand, but they did not understand.*

Just like Moses, you thought for sure that you could do your own thing. You thought that you could stand up for what was right and say, "No guys, this isn't the way things are done. This is wrong."

You thought, "If I could just present these people with the truth and the pattern, they are just going to love it. They're going to say, 'Wow!'"

Do not feel isolated – you are not the only apostle to taste the sting of that rejection.

Letting Go – No Turning Back

When the time comes to "leave Egypt", you cling to the hope that others will understand. There were those in the church that were patting you on the back and saying, "It's great how you can hear from God."

Then the time comes when you leave that church. How many of the congregation picked up the phone to see where you were or how you were doing? How many supported you or even thought of you?

You see, you had to leave them behind. You had to leave everything behind. I know this is a struggle that many face during this phase of preparation, and I have counseled and ministered to so many in the throes of apostolic training.

They have said, "My heart is for the people. I feel for them. If I leave and go off on my own, what about the people? Who is going to take care of them?"

God is quite capable of taking care of His own. You have to let them go. You have to break ties completely and let them go, because you are no good to God where you are right now.

Later, you can return and bring God to the people, but you are no good to man or God where you are right now. You couldn't help them even if you wanted to, because you don't have the equipment, the tools, or the power and anointing yet.

All you are going to give them are empty words, more mindsets and archetypes. You are going to give them more bad templates based on your own preconceived ideas and bad experiences.

You have nothing new to offer them. You may think you have one or two patterns or one or two unique ideas, however, it takes more than a couple of ideas to lead a nation.

It takes more than a couple of good ideas to bring wonders and miracles, and the unexpected into the Church. It takes more than a few ideas to have people respect you and look up to you, so that they will follow you anywhere.

It takes the awesome power of the living God! Until you have the awesome power and anointing of the living God, you have nothing to offer His people. You have no ministry, and you are nothing.

Don't go shouting your mouth off until the words that come out of your mouth are filled with His glory. That is why you are taken to the wilderness. You are on a pilgrimage to find the Holy mountain, to find the glory of God. When you find the glory of God, you will return.

CHAPTER 04

WILDERNESS WANDERINGS

Chapter 04 – Wilderness Wanderings

So I ran away and I dropped everything. What happened next? Here I was sitting in the backside of the desert.

> **Exodus 2:15** *When Pharaoh heard of this matter, he sought to kill Moses. But Moses fled from the face of Pharaoh and dwelt in the land of Midian; and he sat down by a well.*

So Moses fled, sat down by a well and said, "Well, what now Lord? Do I go off and start my own ministry? Do I go off and get involved in another church? Do I go off and start a training center or a mid-week meeting or something, Lord? Surely there has to be something that I can do?"

He said, "Well, go and sit at that well for a while. Then maybe from there, I'll send you to take care of some sheep. For now, just sit down and wait!

"That's it. That's your job. You sit down and shut up and listen for a change, instead of running in five directions all at once. For goodness sakes Moses, you are so busy running around doing your own thing that you can't stop to hear me for five minutes!"

So, He removes all the noise from your life, and now you have no choice. You have no other voices speaking to you, and you have no other ministry leader telling you what to do. You have nobody to even minister to! This is a good place to be, because for the first time in your life you are in a position to hear God's voice more clearly.

The Process Begins

This is where the templates start being smashed. You see, you have to start becoming something new. You have to become a new person, and so, the old must die entirely.

Every link must be broken - every friendship, and every mentorship tie. Everything will be broken and destroyed. There must be absolutely nothing left of who you were, because who you were is not what you will rise up to be when the Lord sends you back.

They will not recognize you when you return. You will not speak in the same way. You will not look the same or minister the same. You will have an entirely different outlook! For this to happen, one by one, every single one of those templates must die!

All your "churchianity" must go. All your ways of doing things and not doing things "by the book" must go, because how can you get a new pattern when you are trying to build that new foundation on an old foundation?

That old foundation is rickety. It has cracks. It has destroyed the church of God and has made it complacent. You cannot build on that foundation. That is why God has taken you out, so that you can build a new one and bring God to the people, and show them the truth and the right way of doing things.

> *Until you can show them the right way of doing things, the old way of doing things must die in you.*

How can you expect them to change when you are not prepared to change yourself?

You want to stand up and give this great speech and tell people how they must live their lives. You want to teach them the Word of God, counsel them, and show them how to do things and how they must change. You want to show them how they must change their view of God, but are you prepared to change your view of God?

You say, "No, I've got it together! I'm the one who has it right here. They are the ones who have it wrong."

Do you think so? Do you think because you have one tiny revelation that you have arrived? Do you know God? Are you perfect yet? If not, then you still have a ways to go.

You need to admit, "Hang on a minute, I don't know God as well as I should. Maybe I don't see things as clearly as I should. Maybe the pattern that I think I have is a pattern that is put together in my mind instead of by inspiration from the Holy Spirit. Perhaps when I stand up, I don't speak under the anointing."

You have to look at yourself and say, "Hang on, am I prepared to do what I'm expecting them to do? Am I prepared to live what I'm expecting them to live?"

You see, Moses goes ahead. The time will come when he will go back and lead the children of Israel through the wilderness. But first, he must go through the wilderness himself.

YOUR METAMORPHOSIS

The Lord showed me this at the very beginning of my apostolic training many years ago. He showed me a vision, which I didn't quite understand at the time, but now it makes such perfect sense!

He showed me that I was going on a journey where I would go down valleys and over mountains. I would walk through very rough terrain, and all I would have with me was a backpack. The journey was mapped out, and I would cut down branches, make bridges. It was a really tough journey. At the end of this journey, I saw myself going back to the starting point.

When I got there, there was a whole group of people waiting. As I walked, some of them followed behind me, and I showed them the way to go.

There were others who were weak, and I had to pick them up and carry them some of the way. Then, there were others who I showed how to build bridges and how to cut down the vines. I showed them how to blaze the trail for themselves.

The Lord showed me how this was my apostolic calling. He showed me how I was to go ahead, go through the training and the preparation, and face those mountains and sheer cliffs. I had to face the valleys. I had to experience the downs of death and the power of resurrection.

I was to go through and experience these things - like the changes and smashing of the templates and mindsets, and the dealings and looking at my motivations and my attitudes.

I was to experience all of this first. Once I had completed this journey, I would then go back to His people. Now having prepared the way, I could take them with me through the wilderness and into the Promised Land.

YOU ONE WHO IS SENT

Before you can lead the children of God anywhere, you need to have gone ahead. That is what apostolic preparation and training are all about.

It is about going ahead, so you can go back and allow God's people to enter into your finished work. You do all the hard stuff – the digging and the travailing and going through the deaths and paying the prices, so that they don't have to.

That is what it means to be a servant, to be the scum of the earth, and to be someone people wipe their feet on. You are going to pay the price so that they do not have to pay it. It is easier for God to get one man to go through all of that than to try to get an entire nation to do it.

You are going to pay the ultimate price, and you are going to cut that path. You will know where you are going, and you will find out the truth so that you can go back and lead them into victory.

DEALING WITH MINDSETS

It is not a stretch to understand then why your first wilderness stop is to deal with your mindsets.

I remember journaling once, and the Lord said to me, "Colette, I'm dealing with all your mindsets right now with regards to ministry."

I said, "Lord, you have to be kidding! I've been out of the church system for years now."

He said, "Yes, you have. You still have mindsets of what a pastor is and what a pastor should be. You have mindsets of how he should be ministering and how you should be ministering. It is still influencing the very way you minister. It has to go."

He did not leave it at that. He also said, "You have negative feelings and wrong templates about certain types of churches because of your bad experiences. It has to go. You cannot afford to have any kind of negative feeling towards any kind of church or any kind of person because I am sending you back in there, and you will go in my power. You cannot afford to have any kind of negativity."

Some of the questions in our apostolic courses ask, "What kind of denomination do you prefer? What kind of denomination do you not want to go to? What kind of music do you like? What kind of music don't you like?"

No Wiggle Room

There is no "wiggle room" for the apostle. You do not have the liberty of "not liking" a certain music style or denomination. You must be versatile. You must be able to listen to every kind of music and sense the anointing (or lack thereof) in it.

You should be able to walk into any church and bring the power of God with you. If you have even a drop of negativity in you towards anything - be it a race, social strata, denomination, or music style - it will prevent you from taking the power of God with you.

You cannot afford to have any prejudice towards any person, any structure, anything, otherwise, you can't go back.

You may say, "Lord, with a push, I can handle the Baptists. The Charismatics are okay. But Lord…. not the Pentecostal Holiness crowd! Lord, don't send me to the Methodists!

"You know what Lord? I could just bring your power to the Charismatics. They would appreciate your power, but Lord don't send me to minister to Catholics or something like that. I couldn't bear it!"

You cannot afford to have a single negativity towards any denomination. You must be prepared to go anywhere, at any time, with the same power, the same conviction, and the same message.

REMOVING PRECONCEIVED IDEAS

So, your wilderness wandering is a time of dealing with those preconceived ideas.

You know the Lord did that with Craig and I. I grew up in South Africa, which was an apartheid nation, where there was segregation of black and white.

I was never really a racist but was brought up in a culture where the blacks were put on one side and the whites on another. Even though I didn't dislike blacks at all, I still held a prejudice.

Whether I liked to admit it or not, that prejudice was still there. You still saw them as less than you, as below you, and as uneducated.

Even though I wasn't racist myself, that is they way I thought because that is what I received from the media, and from being brought up in that society. You were brought up to think with certain prejudices, and you don't even realize it because it is just "normal." You are born and raised there, and so, it is normal for you.

Moses was born in the court and raised there, and so that was just the way things were for him. Then, you go into the wilderness, and you start seeing things a little differently.

And so, the Lord brought us over to Mexico, and I started seeing things from a different perspective.

He opened the doors for us first via the internet. I had people writing to me, and I formed solid relationships with a lot of people who were black. The prejudice was displaced. Now, some of my closest spiritual kids are black. What was foreign to me before is my new normal!

Any prejudice that was there has to be removed because, in the body of Christ, we are of one spirit and of one mind. There is one God and one family. There is no culture. There is no music style, no nationality, and no country or denomination. It is one body in Christ, with one mind, and with one Spirit.

Until you can come to that kind of conviction, you will carry on wandering in the wilderness, year after year, until that is dealt with.

When somebody says to you, "What nationality are you?", and you cannot respond and say, "I belong to the kingdom of God," you are not there yet.

If somebody says to you, "What style of music do you listen to?", and you don't respond, "Anointed music," you are not there yet.

> **We lose our identity in Christ. He is our identity, and He alone is our image.**

How can you stand up behind the pulpit and teach on racism and patriotism if you are not free from these things yourself?

You will not be taken any further. You will not even be released into training until they are dealt with because God cannot place you with your preconceived ideas to lead His Church into another "Dark Age."

He cannot afford for His people to go wandering in the wilderness for another forty years. The end-times are here. It is now. He doesn't have time to mess with mistakes.

This isn't a game. It is not something we do in our spare time. This is the Kingdom and the church of God that is going to shake the foundations of this earth! You are invited to be a significant part of that, or you are invited to put down your staff and forget about the whole thing.

God is not playing games, and He is not messing around. He expects the same commitment from you. He is committed to you to prepare you, shape you, and train you. Are you prepared and committed to Him to allow Him to change you?

TIME OF GROWTH

The wilderness will be the greatest time of your growth. Once you can get over the death and face, "This is what I have to die to, and this is what I have to give up," you can use the wilderness to your own advantage.

What happened with Moses? Look at Exodus 3:1:

> *Now Moses was tending the flock of Jethro his father-in-law, the priest of Midian. And he led the flock to the back of the desert, and came to Horeb, the mountain of God.*

He used the time wisely. He got married and had a couple of sons. He became comfortable there with the priest of Midian. He became friends with him and married his daughter, led his sheep, and established his family. He used the time.

This time is the longest period of your preparation, and you should use it wisely. For myself, this is when I met my husband and had my children.

This is the time that you will spend in business. You will get very caught up with your life. You will start developing your home and start building up your resources. It's likely that you will start being successful in the world and building up and establishing your career. Your ministry will begin to fade.

It will fade into the background where you say, "Yeah, I love the Lord. I'm committed to Him."

You will not turn your back on God. He will always be there, but it won't be the emphasis of your ministry anymore. Some people may not know that you are a Christian anymore, because you don't go around preaching with such fervor anymore.

You think, "Well am I a second-rate Christian now?"

No. The Lord has had to remove you so far from the concept of ministry and church that you will come to the place of not wanting anything to do with it! You may even be considered a backslider by some. In your heart, you love God and know that He has something for you, but you can't do this church thing anymore.

So, you get involved in your daily life. Maybe you will start a business. Maybe you will become involved in climbing up the corporate ladder. You will become successful in the world. You will build up a nice comfortable little structure there.

If you stay as a pastor, perhaps you will pastor a small little flock outside of the system somewhere.

You work during the week, and maybe on Sundays, you go to church. In that silence, and in that working out of your life, those templates are being smashed, one after the other.

You say, "How can that be? I am not doing anything. I'm not ministering to anybody. I don't get it! I don't understand how I can be making progress, and I haven't done anything for years."

What has happened though is that the Lord has corroded all those templates that were in you. He has made them so alien and estranged to what you have become that you can't go back. Your bridges are so well burned that, even if you had to try and go back, you wouldn't fit in.

Perhaps you tried to go back to church once or twice, just to make your spouse happy or have a place for your children to go to, and it just didn't feel right.

If you are hankering back, I invite you to go and give it a try. If you are at the stage where you are hankering back and thinking, "Well why don't I just go back? Maybe it wasn't so bad," then give it a try.

You will soon find out that it is so far removed from what you have become now that you cannot go back. You cannot think that way anymore. You cannot feel that way anymore. You are too restless now. Your feet have begun moving, and they are going to keep moving until you come to the end of this journey.

POSITIVE CHANGE AND TRANSITION

Use the wilderness. This is a perfect time for you to get your life structured and to get your family in order.

> *A butterfly goes through the most change when it is in the cocoon and looks dead.*

You may not be able to see the change in yourself, and others certainly can't see the change in you yet. But, there is change taking place. Don't get stressed. Do not feel that you have to have a goal. Don't feel that you have to force yourself through and go through more training.

Don't think, "I must have an answer, and I must know where I'm going."

Just sit down by the well, shut up, and listen! Just stop all the striving. Relax, and get on with your life. Do the things that you always wanted to. Take up a hobby. When you are relaxed and not thinking about what you do or don't have to do, that is when God can start speaking to you.

The Lord kept telling me something over and over again,

"You know, Colette, you need to have more faith in My ability than you have faith in your own weaknesses and failures."

That really struck me! I had more faith in my own weakness, and in my own ability to fail, than I had in God's ability to reach down to me and pick me up.

I thought that my calling depended on me. I thought that my progress depended on me. I thought it all relied on me, but you know what it really was? It was filthy, rotten pride!

You need to have more faith in God than you have in yourself because then you can sit down by that well, and He will lead the right people across your path. That is what He did with Moses. He said and did the right thing in perfect time and, so, was led to Jethro.

God knows what He is doing even if you don't. Put your trust in Him instead of yourself, and maybe you will start getting somewhere. What have you got to lose? What can happen is that God will reach down and pick you up with His mighty arm, and start you on this road of apostolic preparation.

It says in Acts 7:30:

> And when forty years had passed, an Angel of the Lord appeared to him in a flame of fire in a bush, in the wilderness of Mount Sinai.

CALL TO THE MOUNTAIN

Finally! The call to the mountain arrives. You will be in the travails of death to your flesh. You will be going through all this chiseling of all templates and preconceived ideas.

Then, in the middle of that, the Lord calls you to the mountain! At this stage of the game, you are nothing! You have no passion, you have no desire, and you have no vision for ministry because every last one has been brought to the cross.

You have experienced different denominations. Your temperament has been taken from expressive, to driver, to analytical, to amiable - and all the way back again - and then to a combination of all four. You don't know whether you are being analytical, driving or expressing anymore! You are neither here nor there.

If somebody says, "So what denomination are you?" you say, "To be really honest, I couldn't tell you because I've been in them all."

You don't know what you are. It is like you're dust. Everything you think you are, or thought you were, has been smashed. This is a very good place to be!

> **When what you were no longer exists, what you will become can be raised up out of the ashes.**

God is waiting for that place of nothingness. He is waiting for you to be so sick of ministry, to not even think about ministry or even want to go into it anymore. He is wanting you to come to the place of wandering around aimlessly, getting on with your daily life.

Your heart is towards Him, but you know what? It is a case of, "I have the kids to pick up. I have to take Michael to the soccer game over there. Oh yes, I must remember to pick up the groceries for dinner tonight!"

You are so busy with your daily life that you don't care about ministry anymore!

That is the place God is waiting for you to come to because He can reach in by His grace and His power when you are at that place, and He can lift you up and show you what you are heading for. Until everything has died, you cannot go there.

So you will be raised out of the dust, and the Lord will miraculously draw you to the mountain. He will do it in your weakness, your failure, and your nothingness. His anointing will come upon you, and all the lethargy and all the nothingness and the numbness you felt will vanish in the blink of an eye. A new fire will be lit in you, and a new passion will come.

A Desire to Go Higher

It will be all Him. It will be all His doing. He will come upon you, and He will draw you. You will feel a drawing to go back into the deeper things of God. You will feel a drawing once again that had been dead in you for so long.

Suddenly, you will feel that churning deep inside that says, "I've got to go back! I need more. God, where are you?"

You will suddenly start seeking, and so, the Lord will begin drawing you up the mountain.

This is the place that I had even come to myself. My father had come over to Mexico to found the ministry, and my husband Craig and I were left behind. That is when I faced the bulk of my prophetic training. Before that, it was a case of wandering around. Though I had recommitted my heart to the Lord, I never really had a direction.

It was a case of thinking, "Oh well, I don't know what to do."

Before I had married Craig, I was so put off by this whole churchy thing that I vowed, "I will never marry a pastor!"

As a result, I found the most unpastoral-looking guy I could. He was a metal head with long hair, kitted out in Doc Martin boots, tight jeans, and demonic t-shirts.

I figured, "Hey, you don't get further from a pastor than that, right?"

I brought him home, and my father got him saved. My life was turned upside down from there! The Lord raised my husband up to be a spiritual father and apostle. So there you have it.

The Lord tricked me when I wasn't looking! I had come to that place of nothingness. I had come to that place of where everything had been smashed. I didn't want to know the "pastor thing." I didn't want to know the "church thing." I did not want to know the "Sunday morning meetings thing." I was sick of it all!

God reached in, and said, "Okay, I can do something with you now. Let's get moving!"

He picked me up out of that in the middle of it, and with a sudden shift of events, I landed in Mexico. Suddenly, I was called to the mountain, and my apostolic training proper began.

Changing the Pictures

Until you come to that place of not wanting to go into ministry, or anything to do with it, He can't call you to the mountain. He cannot reveal Himself to you until your preconceived ideas and mindsets are gone.

I was brought up in a really good Christian home with sound principles. However, my mind was still colored with the archetypes of the system, of the world, and of what God was supposed to be.

I didn't know Him as a reality, and God had to remove everything from my life! Whether it was bitterness, preconceived ideas, mindsets, hurts or rejection – whatever it was, I had to deal with all those things before I could meet God for the first time face-to-face.

You see, I knew Him in my head. I knew in my heart that I was saved. Did I know Him as a real living person face-to-face? Did I know Him better than I knew myself?

That is the experience that you will begin having when you encounter God for the first time on the mountain. It is only a starting point. You will only get a glimpse – just a small little bush of what He is.

There is a bit more to be done after that, before you can enter fully into that face-to-face relationship. Before you can even come to the starting point, all that junk needs to be taken away. It needs to be smashed and removed.

Which Stage?

Perhaps it has been prophesied over you that you are an apostle, but there you are, still sitting in church. You are feeling restless and thinking, "There's something more. Things should change."

Is that where you are?

Perhaps you are at the stage where you have already risen up and rocked the boat and have had to run for your life. You have had to leave the system. Perhaps you are in the place of rocking the boat, and there is contention in the church. The pastor is preaching at you from the pulpit, and you don't know what to do.

You are thinking, "I must just escape from this place. I can't handle it."

Perhaps that is where you are.

Perhaps you are at the place where you are ready to leave, or have already left, and you are thinking, "Okay, what now? Where am I? I tried to change things. Lord, I thought I was doing what you wanted me to do, but it didn't work out so well."

Perhaps you are the one sitting in the backside of the desert. You left the system a while ago, and now you are just wandering around. You have left your friends behind. You have left the churches behind, and you are sitting there with nothing.

Perhaps you and your kids spend a bit of time together with your spouse. Maybe that is about it. Maybe you get to read the Word together and sing a couple of songs together. Or, is it just you and the Lord spending a bit of time together in the middle of nowhere?

You are getting on with your life and your career, redecorating your home and putting in new carpeting. Whatever it is, you are not really doing anything. You are just waiting. You are in transition.

Perhaps that part has come to a close, and you are feeling a call towards the mountain.

You are feeling a stirring in you that says, "Enough of this complacency! Enough of this day to day lifestyle. I want more! I've gone through all these deaths. I've gone through all these templates and triggers, and all these issues and bad motivations have been dealt with in me.

"The Lord has taken me from place to place. I've gone from denomination to denomination. I went from job to job, and it has changed my character. I've gone through all of these things. I've dealt with the family issues and friend issues, and all those other things. Now, I want something deeper."

You are feeling a stirring. Perhaps somebody even prophesied it over you. Perhaps you have picked up the Word and received a revelation, and the Lord said, "Come unto me. Come deeper!"

THE CALL

You have a hunger that is growing in you. That is your call to the mountain. It is your call to training, and it is miraculous and divine! It will either come via a prophet prophesying over you, or you will get a direct revelation from God. Perhaps you will get a letter in your email. Or, you will open up the Word, and a scripture will stand out at you and just jolt you.

You will know, "This is my call!"

It will have to be a specific time, and you will have to identify this time because this isn't just any old thing. You have been called to the mountain. There was a time of complacency, and now, suddenly, you have a conviction of, "Now is the time!"

If you cannot identify this time, then you are not there yet. You should be able to mark it on your calendar and say, "This is the time I went into training, when the call to the mountain came. This is when I started going deeper with God."

Your call to the mountain will come when you have let the system go. It will come when all system templates are smashed. It will happen when you have learned to make it in the world and when all your visions for ministry are totally dead. You will have no desire whatsoever for ministry any longer.

When you have fulfilled those criteria, then apostolic preparation comes to an end, and your training will begin. Where are you in this journey? Before you know it, the mountain will stand before you, and the next step you take is one that will change your journey forever.

CHAPTER 05

The Burning Bush Experience

Chapter 05 – The Burning Bush Experience

Exodus 11:4-8 says:

> Then Moses said, "Thus says the Lord: 'About midnight I will go out into the midst of Egypt;
>
> 5 and all the firstborn in the land of Egypt shall die, from the firstborn of Pharaoh who sits on his throne, even to the firstborn of the female servant who is behind the handmill, and all the firstborn of the animals.
>
> 6 Then there shall be a great cry throughout all the land of Egypt, such as was not like it before, nor shall be like it again.
>
> 7 But against none of the children of Israel shall a dog move its tongue, against man or beast, that you may know that the Lord does make a difference between the Egyptians and Israel.'
>
> 8 And all these your servants shall come down to me and bow down to me, saying, 'Get out, and all the people who follow you!' After that I will go out." Then he went out from Pharaoh in great anger.

What a magnificent, powerful leader! However, as we go back and are introduced to Moses as he first encounters the Lord upon the mountain, that is not the leader that we see.

You see, that is where Moses is headed – to that kind of boldness, authority, and presence.

He was headed to the place where he could stand face-to-face with the king of one of the strongest nations, get up in his face and say, "Pharaoh, this is the way it is going to be!"

Before this, Pharaoh had said to Moses, "Get out of here! I will not see your face anymore."

Moses said, "You're right. You will not see my face again, but it is because of my choice – not yours!"

He stood up to such a powerful, strong man who had so many armies behind him that he could have taken Moses out instantly! It was a bit of a change from the Moses we saw on the mountain top, when God first appeared to him through the burning bush.

His change was not instant, but that is where you are headed – to that kind of boldness, courage, and authority.

CONFRONTING PHARAOH WITHIN

Before Moses could stand up and confront the Pharaoh without, he had to confront the Pharaoh within. This is what I want to look at now as we go on this journey.

The greatest obstacle in Moses' way was not Pharaoh, the king of the Egyptians. It wasn't the armies of Pharaoh or the nations that would come against him. It was also not the wilderness, or what he would do once he got into the wilderness.

The greatest obstacle that stood between Moses and accomplishing his mandate was... his fear. Once you can overcome your fear, you can accomplish anything for the kingdom of God!

We begin with Moses in the wilderness. We have had a look at how Moses had gone through this entire preparation in the wilderness, and how he first encountered God on the mountain and came to know Him as a reality.

Moses, however, had become comfortable. He had developed his family. He had a wife and a couple of sons. He was taking care of the sheep and had come to a place of comfort where he said, "I can handle this! I have things under control."

Moses seems very analytical to me. He liked things in control. He liked to have everything where he could have a good look at it, where he could structure it, and where he could say, "Okay, I get up at six in the morning, take the sheep out for a snack, and then I break for lunch. Then, I have a cup of tea."

He liked things in the order they were. It was structured. It was comfortable and felt pleasant for him. Moses didn't get bored doing the same thing day in and day out. He liked it that way, and it was the way he enjoyed living his life.

Then, right in the middle of it, the Lord blew it right out of the water! He appeared to him in the burning bush, and said, "Hey, Moses."

Moses said, "Are you talking to me?"

"Yes, you! It's time for change, Moses. No more comfort zone. No more just plodding along at your own pace. No more being in control of your life, Moses. No more calling the shots and having a nice little structure. It's got to change. Everything must change!"

A Turnaround

> *When you come face-to-face with the Lord and have a divine encounter, you cannot go back to who you were.*

It is over! You tasted something real. You tasted something that had begun to satisfy a deep hunger in you. There was no turning back. From the first time that you encountered God upon the mountain, you knew your life had changed.

You think, "I can't go back to who I was. I can't go back to just being ordinary and complacent and sitting in church every Sunday."

You had tasted something, and the Lord is saying, "Well, do you want it?"

At this stage of the game, you still have a choice.

You can say, "Forget it. I'm not doing this thing!" Or, you can step out and say, "Okay, what's the job?"

That is the valley of decision you are at right now. The Lord will never force His will on you.

He is going to give you a choice and say, "Okay, it's up to you. What is it going to be?"

Are you going to go back to the wilderness to your little sheep, to be nice and comfortable and cozy? Are you going to get off your structure and control, and everything you have become so comfortable with? You need to head out into something that you are not in control of, to something that has no structure and which you cannot see, smell, touch, or hear. It is still all up in the air.

It sounds a bit like Abraham when the Lord came to him and said, "Abraham, head out there."

"Where, Lord?"

"Get your feet moving! I'll tell you when you get there."

That has to mess with an analytical big time!

You may say, "No, but I have to have the whole picture here. If I'm going to be on this road, I need to have it laid out for me. I need to know where the pieces fit into one another. I need to know what my responsibility is and how I'm going to carry it out. When should I be carrying it out? I need to know exactly which direction I'm headed in!"

The Lord says, "Just get your feet moving. No more structure. No more control."

You see, He has to take away your strengths so that you are reliant on Him alone. It is not a comfortable place to be in. But, once you have been there for a couple of years, you get pretty used to it.

Get yourself geared. The structure and the control that you had has to go. From now on, the Lord will be your structure, and He will be your control. He will reveal to you what He wills, when He wills, and how He wills. He will put the pieces together when He wants to do it. You are not in control of your life anymore. The rules have just suddenly changed.

You have begun a journey. You have entered through a door, and you cannot ever go back. You can try, but you cannot go back to the wilderness. You have tasted something more. You have seen that burning bush, and you know there is something else out there.

So, Moses was confronted with God saying, "Moses, I'm sending you back to Egypt."

"What!? Egypt?"

Fearful Thoughts

What was the first thing that came to Moses' mind? He closed his eyes and went back, and saw himself killing the Egyptian.

He saw how his own brothers turned against him and said, "Who do you think you are, Moses? Do you think you are a self-proclaimed deliverer? We didn't ask you to come and deliver us. We didn't ask you to stand up and protect us. Get out of here! We don't need you."

He remembered Pharaoh finding out what he had done, and the fear that had gripped him. He thought about the soldiers coming for his life, and how he had grabbed what he had and ran out of there. He felt the fear, the insecurity, and the rejection. He remembered how everything had just fallen apart.

When Moses thought of Egypt, this is what came to his mind - everything he failed at and everything he did wrong. He was an outcast! Whether his intentions were good enough or not, it didn't matter.

He said, "I must go back to that?"

What was Moses' greatest fear? God had said to him, "This is it, Moses. I'm sending you back!" In Exodus 3:13 it says:

> *Then Moses said to God, "Indeed, when I come to the children of Israel and say to them, 'The God of your fathers has sent me to you,' and they say to me, 'What is His name?' what shall I say to them?"*

Then it says in Exodus 4:1:

> *Then Moses answered and said, "But suppose they will not believe me or listen to my voice; suppose they say, 'The Lord has not appeared to you.'"*

His greatest fear was not Pharaoh. It was not all the armies in Egypt. Moses' greatest fear was facing God's people. He didn't seem to think that facing Pharaoh would be much of a trouble with God behind him. His greatest fear was facing God's people - the very ones he was going to deliver.

Why did he fear them so much? It was because Moses was insecure. He had faced so much rejection that he didn't want to go back and face that rejection again.

Moses was still thinking with the mind of a spiritual child. He was thinking like he did before he left Egypt. He thought about what a failure he was, how he messed up, and how nobody understood him. That is what he was remembering, and in his eyes, that was still how he saw himself. He was, "Little Moses."

You see, what Moses did not realize was that he had spent forty years in the wilderness. During that time, the Lord had started changing him. Bit by bit, the Lord had started shaping him, dealing with those insecurities and fears.

In his mind, however, he was still thinking like a child. In his mind, he was still thinking like a failure, and he could still see the rejection. He could still hear the snide remarks, and he still shuddered at the reactions he got from the people back then.

He thought, "Oh Lord, I can't do that. I can't speak. I can't handle it. I can't handle that rejection again and be a failure!"

Sometimes, apostolic preparation is like that. You feel like everything you touch fails. You feel like everything you do goes wrong. It is one failure after the next, and you come to the Lord eventually, and say, "Am I going to get anything right?"

Eventually, you just come to the conclusion that, that is the way it is.

You say, "I just mess up! I'm never going to get there."

You get to that place of giving up, of just being a nobody in the backside of the desert. You stop trying entirely. Then God raises you up, and says, "That's it. I'm sending you back."

Your first thought is, "What if I mess it up again? What if I fail again? What if I get my hopes up, get stirred up and excited, and get passionate and head out for this goal, just for it to dissolve in my hands again? I don't know if I can face that kind of disappointment. I don't know if I can face that kind of rejection and letdown. It would destroy me."

Moses had to face that possibility of failure, of disappointment, and of not making it again. After all these years, he had to face the possibility that they would not accept his word.

Isn't that how it was with a lot of prophets in the Old Testament? I think Jeremiah had it the worst!

The Lord said to him, "Jeremiah, I have a word for you to give my people, but just so you know ahead of time, they are not going to listen to you. They will not even care what you have to say! You are going to warn them, and they are not going to heed my word one little bit.

"In fact, it will be so bad, Jeremiah, that you will be an outcast for it, and they are going to punish you for it. You're going to have a pretty lousy life, but hey, stand up and preach it anyway. I'm with you!"

I think Jeremiah had a huge amount of commitment because I don't think I could do that. He knew they were going to reject him outright.

Now here, Moses stood in this uncertainty. He said, "If I go out there, I could mess this up because I messed up last time. What is going to make this time any different?"

God's Representative

I tell you what will make this time different. This time, you will not be going as "Colette Toach." You are not going as you. You are going as a representative of Almighty God! You are going as Jesus. You are not going as you, in your own strength or ability. You are going in His.

It has taken the Lord a long time to bring you to this place of weakness.

> *It has taken Him a long time to bring you to this place of humbling, so that you will be ready to carry such an honor upon your shoulders.*

This is what makes this time more different than anything else. It is because it is not you going out there. It is Him going out there.

Do you know what? God never messes up! He doesn't fail or have disappointments. The Scripture says that every word that proceeds out of the mouth of God goes forth and accomplishes that for which it was sent, and it does not return void.

He doesn't make bad plans. He doesn't make mistakes or errors. He doesn't have a flaw in His pattern. So, when He implements a pattern, it works the first time.

You have to come to the place of trust like you have never trusted anyone in your life! You come to where you are leaning on Him and Him alone, because that is all you have to hold onto. When you go out to confront Pharaoh and the system, you will be going out with the Lord's strength and not your own. When you can overcome this first obstacle of your own fear of disappointment and fear of failure, you are one small step towards that goal.

It comes with death to your fears and with saying, "Lord, I cannot do this! I'm afraid that I'm going to fail. I'm afraid that I am going to let you down. However, I'm prepared to do this."

It is an attitude thing. It is a heart thing. You don't have to be educated to do this, nor do you need to be well-trained to do it. You don't need to have so many strengths to accomplish the task. No. You just need obedience.

You just need a heart that is prepared to say, "Okay, I don't know what's ahead of me. I don't know if I can do this. If you want me to do it God, then I'm prepared to do it."

It is a commitment of your heart. That is all God is asking for. He is not asking for you to do the signs and wonders yourself. He is just asking you to commit your heart to it. When you can commit your heart to it, that is when His hand can be released to move on your behalf.

Why It's Different

Moses had to step out there on his own, and he remembered the last time he did that. It terrified him! He said, "I can't do this on my own. I can't speak!"

What did God say to Moses? He said to him in Exodus 4:19:

> *Now the Lord said to Moses in Midian, "Go, return to Egypt; for all the men who sought your life are dead."*

He said, "Hey Moses, stop sweating about it! It's not the same anymore."

His mind was still caught in the past though, and in his failure. It was still on the image of that young lad who messed up so badly.

It is like being the dropout at school and being the unpopular kid, but you can grow up and be successful in the world. You rise up to be the Managing Director of a huge company! However, no matter how successful you are, when you think back on your school days, that same feeling of insecurity grips you because you remember the children teasing you.

You remember being picked on. You remember being unpopular and failing in school, or whatever it was that your weakness was. When you think back on those memories, you still feel like that child.

There are many people who say, "I wish I could go back with what I know now."

OLD INSECURITIES ARE STILL THERE

If you had to go back, you would still feel the same way. You would still be just as insecure, and just as inferior, no matter how many degrees you have behind your name.

No matter how much you have risen up in this world and proved to everybody from your parents down to the class bully what you can do and are capable of doing, when you think back, you are still a child. You are still insecure and still feel inferior.

It is as though God is saying, "I'm sending you back to school. I'm sending you back to that time where you were picked on and where you were the outcast. You are going back there.

Not only am I sending you back in there, but I'm sending you in there to lead them. Everybody who picked on you, looked down on you, and called you stupid – I'm calling you to be their leader."

Moses said, "They are not going to believe me."

Why did he say that? It was because, in his mind, he was still thinking as that insecure child.

God says to you, "Okay, it is time for you to head out. It is time for you to start confronting the system. I have put you in the wilderness for long enough. You need to go in there and start doing what I have called you to do."

The first thing that grips your heart is, "I can't do this! What if they see through me? What if they see what I really am?"

So let's look at that - what are you really? You are seeing yourself as that child. You are afraid that if you go back out there, that is what they are going to see as well.

What you haven't realized is that the Lord has taken you from image to image, from glory to glory, and that child as you knew it has long since changed. You are now standing as an adult in His glory - with His mantle, His power, and His authority. Now when those people look at you, that is what they are going to see.

That is not what you see, however. You see your insecurity.

Leave the Past Behind

Can't you see that it is in your own eyes? That is not what they are going to see, and that is not what God sees. He sees somebody who He is going to raise up to carry His mantle of authority, anointing, and power. You have to let go of the past. You have to let go of that child, those feelings of inferiority, and that insecurity, hurt, and rejection.

That image has gone. It is over! From the time you stepped up that mountain, the past is gone. The links and the cords are finished! It never happened.

I discussed this aspect in *The Pharaoh You Know*, and how the Lord has been slowly dealing with those things in you. Over a period of time, He has dealt with the templates. He has dealt with the hurts. He has dealt with the rejection. As you have come into the presence of the Lord on the top of the mountain and entered into that relationship with Jesus, He has begun to heal those hurts.

The pictures, however, are still there. You don't realize that that weakness is not in you anymore. It is over. It is not there. Perhaps in the memories and pictures of your mind, the weakness is still there.

You have to let go of those pictures. You have to let go of those memories and take the Lord at His Word. If He considers you ready for this, then you must be ready for it! The past is over. The image that was is smashed. It doesn't exist anymore.

The "Colette" that was doesn't exist anymore. It never happened because a new image is being formed on top of the mountain. It is the first of many images to come. The old is history! Stop living in the past!

> *Stop living in the archetypes, the mindsets, and the pictures of the past. Until you can let them go, you cannot move forward.*

I don't care what you went through to get here or what you have faced in your life. I don't care what your experiences were. I don't even care about what teaching you received and what programming you received. Up until this point, it is gone. It never happened.

It may have formed a foundation in you, but it's over. This season is completed, and until you can let it go, the new vision cannot be resurrected.

SOMEONE TO LEAN ON

Moses, the leader of Israel, needs to come up from the ashes, and Moses, the failure, needs to stay in the ashes. You need to lay down the failure and the weakness in the ashes, and allow the Lord to raise you up as a true leader for His people in His glory.

God was gracious, and He heard Moses. He could see that he was having a really tough time with it. So, He gave Moses somebody to go along with him.

You say, "Lord, I can't handle this by myself. I feel weak. I feel insecure."

He says, "Okay."

You can handle something if you just have somebody else there with you. They don't need to help you. They don't even need to do the task for you. Just to have somebody there helps you to get through the tough things in life. You feel that if you have somebody's hand to hold onto, you can face the future. You can do this thing.

You say, "Lord, if just one person can listen to me, I know that maybe I'm not missing it so badly."

ENTER... AARON

So, the Lord sent Aaron to Moses. It says in Exodus 4:27-30:

> *And the Lord said to Aaron, "Go into the wilderness to meet Moses." So he went and met him on the mountain of God, and kissed him.*
>
> *28 So Moses told Aaron all the words of the Lord who had sent him, and all the signs which He had commanded him.*
>
> *29 Then Moses and Aaron went and gathered together all the elders of the children of Israel.*
>
> *30 And Aaron spoke all the words which the Lord had spoken to Moses. Then he did the signs in the sight of the people.*

The Lord sent Moses somebody who would be under him, who believed in him. That is all Moses needed. He just needed one person to believe in him. This is where your family comes into play. You see, for Moses, it was his brother.

In some cases, it will be a spouse – your husband or your wife. It may be your children, or your parents, but there will be somebody there who will understand. The Lord will send you somebody. He is gracious. He will not leave you to face the wolves by yourself. He knows that you are capable, but He also knows that you just need that support.

That is why the apostolic team concept, and the apostolic family, is so vital at this stage in your training - if, for nothing else, they are just there to say, "We believe in you," when the whole world looks as though it doesn't believe in you.

When the mountain seems larger than life, and you don't think you can ever climb it, there is somebody next to you to say, "I bet you could climb that mountain in ten seconds flat! I bet you could level it!"

You go, "No way! I don't think I could do that."

"I bet you could. I'm telling you. I know you could take that mountain with one hand behind your back!"

You only need one person to have confidence in you, and to believe in you. I thank the Lord that I have a husband who does that. I know that I couldn't climb the mountain. I couldn't confront Pharaoh, and I couldn't go out and do what God has called me to do if I didn't at least have that.

He comes to me before every message and says, "Go knock 'em dead! Be powerful. Be anointed. Be full of the Spirit. You're gonna do this!"

When I say, "Man I can't believe I did that," he says, "I knew you would do it!"

He has greater faith in me than I have in myself, and it inspires me to keep going because somebody understands. I don't need him to do the work for me. I just need him to be there, to understand, and to support me.

You can take on the biggest mountain, the biggest Goliath, and the meanest Pharaoh when you have just one person who stands by your side!

YOU NEED THAT SUPPORT

This can make or break your ministry. If your husband or your wife is not standing with you at this stage of your calling, then stop right there because you are not going to make it. You will not make it unless you have at least one person standing with you.

It does get tough. You will get a lot of opposition. When you get that opposition, you need at least one person for confirmation to say, "That revelation you got was right on! The Lord has confirmed it to me. The direction you are going in is of God. I feel good in my spirit about this."

It is important to have that protection of fellowship and covering when it seems the whole world is against you.

Moses was facing Pharaoh, and the children of Israel were getting angry at him because now they were forced to do extra work. Pharaoh was against him, his servants were against him, and all the elders were against him - but Aaron remained.

He was still there to say, "Moses, God told you to do this. I know He told you to do this. Let's press on through. Let's do this thing and follow it through!"

When it feels like the world is falling apart, you think, "Did I hear God right? Lord, I must be in deception because everybody else says I'm in deception, and everybody else says I'm missing it. They're calling me arrogant and proud. They're saying that I'm out of order. Am I missing it? Did I really hear from you God, or was this me?"

You need that one person to say, "Press on. Push through. God told you to do that, and I believe in you. I believe in what God has told you."

That is all you need. If you don't have that, you are not going to make it. You will not make it because a human being can only take so much affront and rejection on their own, and then they fall. You have to have somebody at your back, leaning against you, that you can lean against, so that you can hold each other up.

That is why your husband or your wife is such a vital part of your ministry. If they do not stand with you, you cannot even go into apostolic training. It should be dealt with at apostolic preparation.

They don't have to go ahead of you. They don't have to be mightier or more anointed. They just have to be there for you to lean on. They just have to believe in you, that's all.

Aaron's Strength

That is your Aaron - and we thank the Lord for the Aarons in our lives who are there to cover our weaknesses. Moses hid behind Aaron a lot.

When they first went to speak to Pharaoh, Moses hid behind Aaron. Instead of Moses making the initial speeches, it was Aaron who was the big, bold speaker.

It was Aaron who did the first signs and wonders as well. It was Aaron who spoke on behalf of Moses continually.

When Aaron and Moses met, the Lord said, "Tell Aaron that you are like God to him, and he is as your prophet."

Moses would tell Aaron what to say, and it was Aaron who was the big, strong leader that said everything.

Moses Makes the Transition

Let's fast forward a bit to the passage in Exodus 11:4. From hiding behind Aaron, we find a bold Moses who does not compromise his stand.

What happened? What happened is that, as Aaron was confronting Pharaoh with Moses standing behind, every now and again, he stuck his head in and got a word in edgewise. Every now and again, he thought, "Hey, I can handle this," and so he started getting out there and testing the waters.

Moses started discovering, "Hang on a minute. I can do this thing. Hang on. I'm not such a failure!"

God had given him signs and wonders, and they had proved themselves.

He thought, "Hey, I'm not a weakling! God has placed His anointing on me, and it has been proved time and time again with every plague that came upon Egypt."

The anointing that was on Moses was proved, not just in the sight of the people, not just in the sight of Pharaoh, but in the sight of Moses. When Moses finally came to the place of getting over the fear described in that first passage, where he could confront Pharaoh himself, the children of Israel were released instantly.

We think that the ten plagues that came upon Egypt were just for the benefit of the Egyptians, and for the children of Israel. It was not so. They were also for the benefit of Moses.

You see, Moses needed to know in his own heart that he was called. He needed to get over his own fear and his own insecurity. The only way that God could get him over those things was for him to go out there and prove the anointing that was on him.

With every miracle that came to pass, and with everything that happened as Moses spoke it, his confidence began to grow.

With each time you face your fear and confront it, you overcome it more and more until it is no longer a fear. Each time Moses came into the presence of Pharaoh and confronted that fear continually by having it in his face, he came to the place where he could not only look at this fear, but where he could get angry and say, "Don't you dare! Now you listen to me. I'm in charge here."

THE VICTOR

He didn't only overcome it, but he conquered it. He was a victor over it, and he said, "Pharaoh, don't talk to me like that. Who do you think you are? I speak on behalf of God, and I say what goes! I say that you will not see my face again, and I say that the firstborn in all of Egypt will die.

"Look at me, Pharaoh! You will know that I have been speaking for God. You will know that there is a distinction between Egypt and Israel. You will know the mighty God I serve, and you will tremble! Your servants will come to me and tell me that I can go. I am not going to grovel to you any longer and beg you any longer. You will come to me from this time forward!"

Moses had the victory. He had gotten a conviction. Suddenly, the passion and the vision took a hold of him. It was right there. He could taste it in his mouth, and nothing could stand in his way. He was finally ready to leave Egypt, to head out now on the mandate that God had called him to.

Perhaps you are looking at this whole thing and saying, "There are so many obstacles in the way."

I painted a very bleak picture for you earlier of that image of a child. You know the only way you are going to overcome it is not by hiding in the wilderness and thinking about it. It is by getting up in the face of your fear and confronting it.

You have to confront your fear again and again! You cannot keep running away from it for the rest of your life because it is going to stay there until you have conquered it. Once you have conquered it, you will walk through. Once you walk through it, you can begin walking out the calling that is on your life.

The greatest obstacles that are between you and accomplishing the mandate that God has given you are your fears, your insecurities, and your feelings of inferiority.

These are the things that stand in the way. When you have overcome those, the rest will just be a matter of walking out the calling that God has put before you.

It is not God who is holding you back. It is not Him who has even put those obstacles in your path. They have always been there. He is calling you beyond the obstacles. If you can rise up beyond them, you are going to start seeing miracles happening in your life! It will be a matter of night and day, and God will release you into what He has called you to be.

CHAPTER 06

CONFRONTING PHARAOH

Chapter 06 – Confronting Pharaoh

Without realizing it, you have been going through a transformation – a renewal of your mind. The fears that hounded you in the past have left, and you wonder in amazement at the silence you have in your mind now!

Where before, you were always thinking the impossible. God had to take you and shake you by the shoulders to say, "Begin to see through my eyes of possibility."

Enter… Joshua

In Scripture, we can see that Joshua began to see things as Moses saw them. He looked at this great big land with all these giants, and he saw the possibilities.

He said, "Yes sure, they are giants. But hey guys, this is the land that God's given us."

He began to see as Moses saw, but that is not how Moses started out. Moses started out saying how much could go wrong.

He said, "Lord, here's a list of why I shouldn't go back to Egypt. Here's why it won't work."

He had all the impossibilities down from point 1 to 10, A – Z, but God said, "I'm messing with your plans, Moses. From today, I'm not only smashing your image, but I'm also smashing the way you think. I am taking you from impossibility thinking to possibility thinking. I want you to look past the giants and past your fear."

> **Look past Pharaoh, all his armies, and all the children of Israel, and see the possibilities before you.**

SEE IT

Moses apostle, what if you really pull this thing off? Imagine with me for a minute. What if you actually do go out there, and the anointing does come on you? What if you go out there and speak, and people actually do hear the message that you have to bring and really do change? What if you step out there, and they really follow after what you are saying, and the Church changes?

What if mighty warriors begin to rise up because of what you have to say? What if the fire in them is ignited, and the power of God comes on these people? What if signs and wonders begin happening in the homes of everyday believers?

Well, now... you will never know until you get out there and try.

You have the potential to lead God's people to the Promised Land – to break the Church free of the religion and bondages that have been there for centuries.

To bring the anointing that causes the scales to fall off the eyes of every believer, so that they might rise up to see the truth and enter into a real relationship with Jesus.

You can stay here in your comfort zone and sit and think, "What if I fail? What if they say, 'Who do you think you are?'"

If you are going to sit, thinking about those "what ifs", then you are never going to leave the wilderness! If you are going to keep filling your mind with the impossibilities, you will not go anywhere.

On the other hand, if you can start filling your mind with the hundreds of possibilities that await you, the Lord can begin working with you.

When your mind is renewed with His possibility thinking, you will step out with His anointing, and by His command.

Faith Required

You will be stepping out there in faith. Without faith, it is impossible to please God. You see, God isn't expecting you to be perfect. He is not expecting you to get it all right. He is not going to grade you on your success ratio, on how many people listen to you and how many don't.

He doesn't care! He wants one thing from you - faith in Him. He wants you to have faith that He will accomplish His Word in you. He just wants your faith and your commitment. With faith, comes obedience.

When you trust somebody, you will listen to them, won't you? You'll do what they say. That is all He expects of you.

When you can put yourself in His hands and say, "Okay, I believe you. I can do this. I trust you, Lord," then He can begin doing something with you. He will send you out in His power.

It is just faith He requires. How much skill did it take to look after a couple of sheep? The rest of the leadership ability came later on. All that God needs at this stage in the game is your faith and your obedience. He doesn't need you to be a great speaker or a great leader.

He does not need you to be anything other than obedient. He will do the rest. Then as He works out those signs and wonders one at a time, and as your ministry is proven again and again, you will begin to grow confident. Then, you will grow into that leader.

I shared in *The Key of David* book the changes that the Davidic apostle goes through from shepherd boy to king. You don't start out as King. You don't start out as Moses, the great leader. You start out as Moses the shepherd, very much like David started out as the shepherd.

You see, all God is wanting from you is that obedience and faith. As you take that first step forward, the transformation will begin to take place from image to image. After Moses went through this transformation, you see him all up on Pharaoh's face! He was not cowering in the backside of the desert, but right up there where the action was.

Suddenly, the possibility thinking was a reality. It was now a case of, "What if I go there, and the people listen to me?"

Not only did the people hear Moses, but they rejoiced. They said, "God has heard our affliction! You're sent of God. Moses, you're the answer to our prayers! We've been praying for you, Moses."

You see, if Moses hadn't gone out, he would never have known that they were on their faces before the Lord saying, "Lord, send us a deliverer."

THE ANSWER TO PEOPLE'S PRAYERS

Moses was the answer to their prayers, however he would never have known that if he had walked away saying, "What if they don't listen? What if I fail?"

> ***Exodus 4:30*** *And Aaron spoke all the words which the Lord had spoken to Moses. Then he did the signs in the sight of the people.*
>
> *31 So the people believed; and when they heard that the Lord had visited the children of Israel and that He had looked on their affliction, then they bowed their heads and worshiped.*

They said, "Thank you, Lord!"

You know, you might be surprised to go out there and hear people saying, "I've been praying to God for this. I have been waiting my whole life for somebody to come up to me and just tell me what my place is!

"I've been waiting all my life for somebody to show me that there's something more. I've been praying earnestly to encounter the Lord in a new way and to develop a relationship with Him that I've never had, and you're giving that to me."

"I've prayed my whole life for my marriage to be restored, and for my family to be restored. Now that you've come and shared the message that God has given you, these things have happened."

Your True Purpose

Don't you realize that you will be the answer to the prayers of many men and women? Do you think God is sending you out for your own good? No. He has raised you up, and He is sending you because of the cry of His people.

You are an answer to their prayer. If you do not go, and if you do not confront the fear of rejection and the Pharaoh in your life, who is going to be the answer to their prayer? Who is going to go and meet their need?

Are you just going to leave them there to remain slaves for the rest of their lives, in bondage to the system? Will you leave them there to suffer? Are you going to leave them to think that God has left them and doesn't care about them anymore?

If you are an apostle, I should hope not. I should hope you care a little bit more than that, otherwise, you wouldn't be an apostle, would you? It burns in you to see change! It burns in you to bring God to the people, to show them that reality. All that stands in your way is your fear.

Pharaoh is nothing! He can be drowned in the sea in an instant. It is the Pharaoh within you that is the greatest obstacle. It is you that is in the way, apostle. It's not the world or the system. It's not the people.

> **It is you that is in the way of your own calling.**

You see, when the power of God comes on you and the anointing is on you, there is no king and no nation that can stand before that because the mountains tremble at the voice of Almighty God. The Red Sea parted at just a breath of His nostrils.

Accomplishing the task is the easy part because it is the Lord that does it with His power and anointing. That is not the greatest obstacle. The greatest obstacle is getting over "you." When you can get yourself out of the way, God can do something, and He can use you.

When you look in the mirror, the greatest obstacle is the Pharaoh within your own heart. You can overcome him just by facing and confronting him.

LATER... IS NOW

You have been running and hiding all your life saying, "I'll deal with that later!"

I hate to break it to you, but later has caught up with you! You are facing "later" right now. You can't run anymore. You can't pretend it is not there anymore. It is being put right in your face.

You're saying, "It is too painful. I can't face that rejection. I do not want to feel or look at my shame. You should have heard the names that they called me. Even now when I hear that name, I shudder and it hurts inside. So, I don't want to talk about it. If somebody brings it up, I just change the subject."

The Lord is saying, "No. You face it and deal with it now because you are not going anywhere until you have overcome."

You cannot overcome out there until you have overcome what is within you. It is a mountain in front of you that seems impossible to climb! But you know what? With just a flick of His finger, it is gone. It is up to you to confront that mountain.

You are not going to confront it alone. You are going to do it with those whom God has brought into your life, and you are going to confront it with the power of Almighty God. You will face it with the Word of God and with the anointing, and now, as an adult, not as a child.

You forget, apostle, that spiritually speaking you are not a young insecure, little teenager anymore. You are now a spiritual adult. It is time to stop thinking as a child, and start thinking as an adult.

THE PRICE OF THE CALL

I want you to look at the price of the Moses apostolic calling. The first price you must pay is obedience, regardless of what you have to face or of whether it makes sense or not.

You should be saying, "Okay, you're God. I'm the human here. I will obey."

The second price you will pay is to face your fears. You will face the Pharaoh within you.

The third price, and the final step you will take to completing your mandate, is stepping out in faith.

I want you to make a recommitment in your heart to this thing now.

Say, "Okay Lord, I'm tired of running. You know how much I've failed. You alone really know my weaknesses. Lord, there is some stuff I haven't even told my husband or wife. These things are so deep within me that I have even forgotten them because I don't want to look at them.

"I didn't want to look at my failure or my weakness. I didn't want to face that rejection again Lord. It hurts too much. When I think about the things they said, about how I messed up and what happened as a result of it, Lord, I just don't know if I can face this."

I want you to know that you are facing this with the Lord. You can do this thing. You can face this fear once and for all, and you can overcome it!

I want you to face your fear and say, "In the name of Jesus, I will overcome you! In the name of Jesus, mountain you will be removed! The Word says, 'Whoever says to this mountain be removed and cast into the sea, and does not doubt in his mind, but believes in his heart that those things that he says shall come to pass, he shall have whatever he says.'

"Mountain, be removed and cast into the sea. Insecurity, fear of rejection, and fear of man, be removed and cast into the sea. Inferiority, be removed and cast into the sea.

"Hurt, pain, shame, bitterness, be removed and cast into the sea. I smash you! I divide you. I walk through you, in the name of Jesus Christ. I am covered in His Blood. I am standing in His armor, and you will not get in my way any longer. You will not hinder me.

"I will say to you, 'Pharaoh…. let God's people go!'"

Rise up, apostle of God, and take up the mandate that is on your life.

Chapter 07

Climbing the Mountain

Chapter 07 – Climbing the Mountain

You have taken a step of faith and embraced your call. As much as I have levied some strong challenges at you, you remain here in Chapter 7, ready to know what the next steps are that you need to take.

Now that you have confirmed your calling, let's take another step towards what you can expect the Lord to do as you answer that call.

In fact, from the moment that you say, "Yes Lord! I accept this call to apostleship. I am ready to pay any price," you will find a mountain looming ahead of you with the voice of the Lord saying, "Come to the mountain."

I know that many people have even had dreams and visions where the Lord has said to them, "Climb up and meet me at the top of My mountain."

In this chapter, I would like to share with you from the Word, and from experience, what I believe is the Lord's word for us at this time. I will share what climbing the mountain means for you as an apostle, what it means for the body of Christ, and what it means for you in your personal life.

How You Receive the Mountain Call

> *1 Corinthians 13:8 Love never fails. But whether there are prophecies, they will fail; whether there are tongues, they will cease; whether there is knowledge, it will vanish away.*
>
> *9 For we know in part and we prophesy in part.*
>
> *10 But when that which is perfect has come, then that which is in part will be done away.*

I would like to begin by looking at exactly what the mountain is that the Lord will call you to during your training. What is the mountain? What does it represent in the apostolic calling?

To put it very simply, the mountain is a time of separation. You are going to experience this sooner or later in your walk. Perhaps, by the end of this chapter, you will be able to gauge where you are in this process.

A UNIQUE CALL

There needs to come a time of separation from the world. This is where the Lord can draw you to Himself for a time of intimate training, change, teaching, and a face-to-face relationship.

You cannot move fully into the apostolic office until you have had this time of separation. This is because until you are able to hear the Lord's voice for yourself, you cannot move into all that He has for you.

If you, standing as an apostle and leader in the body of Christ, are not able to hear the Lord's word clearly and precisely, and know exactly which step to take next, you are not going to make it as a leader.

At the first sign of opposition or deception, you are going to fall.

So, this time is probably the central point of your apostolic training. It will dictate where your ministry is going to. It will show you what function your ministry will have and what track you are going to run on.

Even now, I can already see you starting to put the pictures together in your mind.

You are likely thinking to yourself, "I wonder what that means to me? I wonder what the Lord is going to show me? I wonder what track He is going to put me on?"

It is important that you think in this way because every apostle is different. Although our training is similar, each one of us is unique in the way the Lord has brought us to this point. You are unique in the way you think, speak, and minister. There is a pattern just for you!

A Solitary Climb

> *Your apostolic training will kick off with a call to the mountain.*

You need to have a time of solitude. One of the first conditions of climbing the mountain is that you climb alone. This is very important because there comes a time of confusion where you feel that everybody has left you, and that you are the only one still going on. You feel alone and isolated.

Perhaps this is the Lord calling you aside to that time of separation because when you climb up the mountain, you climb alone. Nobody can tell you how to climb, and nobody can tell you how to hear the voice of the Lord.

These are things that you, as an apostle, have to learn for yourself because until you have learned them, you cannot teach them to others.

Until you can hear His voice, you cannot tell the people, "Thus says the Lord ..."

Until you have received direction, you cannot lay out the pattern for the people. So, you climb alone. It is a lonely, and sometimes, misunderstood walk.

You need to realize that if this is what you are facing in your life right now, this could very well be the Lord saying, "I am calling you to the mountain. Let it go and come aside alone with me so that I can share with you."

A Pull to Get into the Spirit

You need to be taken out of your natural circumstances. You need to be taken away from the things that influence you every day and get into the spiritual realm.

When you are going to work, when the kids are nagging you, or your spouse is giving you a tough time, it is very difficult to get in the Spirit.

When your boss is yelling at you, and you are having pressure from all external influences, it is not easy to walk in the Spirit. It is not very easy to hear the Lord's voice.

That is why this time of separation is so vital. It is to shut off all the external stimuli that is pressing down on you. It serves to silence the noise attacking your mind that is confusing the message that the Lord is trying to share with you.

The only way that you can get away from it is in a time of complete separation, perhaps even a time of fasting and prayer. The Lord will pull you totally away from all your natural senses, templates, daily schedules - everything that imposes any kind of external influence on you from without.

If this is happening to you right now, then be encouraged. The Lord is putting you into a special, secret place - a place where He is going to build you up to be a magnificent leader for the kingdom of God!

But you must realize that you have to be pulled out of the natural. You cannot remain having those natural things coming at you and still receive the Spirit of the Lord.

HEARING HIS VOICE

Up until now, you have not been able to hear His voice quite as clearly as you should be hearing it. As a prophet, if you have moved in the prophetic ministry, you have come to a degree of hearing His voice and speaking in prophecy. But there comes a deeper level in the apostolic ministry when you move beyond speaking "for the Lord" to speaking "as the Lord." I will explain on this a bit more. It does not mean you take God's place, but rather that you are so in tune with the spirit that, as you speak, you feel God's words bubbling out of you. You no longer need to say,

"Thus saith the Lord." Rather, you are speaking with wisdom, and it is clear God is speaking through you!

The words that you speak as an apostle are very important. Your words bear on the situation, so you had better speak right! You cannot afford mistakes when standing as a leader in the kingdom of God.

A Clean Slate

There is another condition that is probably more difficult than being pulled out of your natural surroundings. This relates to the fact that, when you go up the mountain, you cannot take anything of this world with you.

When Moses climbed the mountain, he did not take his tent, his wife, or his cattle. He didn't even take any food and water! At least we have it good and get to keep our food and water.

He left everything that he was, everything that he had, and everything that he had accomplished in this life. Even the people that he was leading were left behind. He could not even take them up! He had to leave them to their own devices.

> **As you go to the top of the mountain, you will not be able to take your degrees, your doctorates, or your great leadership skills.**

You are not going to be able to take your great ability to influence people with emotion. You will not be able to take up your great big shows of supremacy and your ability to speak well. You cannot take them with you. God sees right through that.

You are not going up there to seek the face of man. You are going up there to seek the face of God, and He does not look at what degrees you have. He does not look at how well you speak or how magnificent you are. He looks at your heart.

If you think you are going to approach God with, "Oh Lord, I'm such a great leader, and look what wonderful things I've done in your kingdom," expect to trip over the first stone! Your accomplishments are one of the first things you are going to leave behind.

You are coming to God on your hands and knees and with your face on the ground. That is how you are coming to God, as Moses did, in humility. You are not coming with your great speech and eloquence. You are not coming with all the accomplishments that you have done in the kingdom of God.

In fact, I will tell you this now by the Spirit of God. Take everything that you have done in ministry and your life up until this point, and scratch it! This is because before the mountain and after the mountain are two different lives.

Take everything you have accomplished in ministry, and everything you have accomplished in life, and just sweep it to one side because it does not exist anymore. When you come down from the mountain, the old you will not exist anymore, therefore, that old life will not exist anymore.

You are coming down in new glory! You are coming down in power!

> *Do not expect that what worked before is going to work now. You are going to come down a different kind of leader.*

WHY YOU RECEIVE THE MOUNTAIN CALL

> ***1 Corinthians 2:9*** *But as it is written: "Eye has not seen, nor ear heard, nor have entered into the heart of man the things which God has prepared for those who love Him."*

Why do you need the mountain? You need to get into the Spirit, apostle of God. You need to put away the soulish mind, because the soulish man does not perceive the things of the Lord.

To Receive the Mind of Christ

You cannot approach this with your mind. This is not something you can comprehend with intellectual thinking. This goes way deeper than the mind! It goes into the Spirit. For you to touch the spiritual realm of God, you have to bring your spirit into control to dominate your flesh and your soulish mind. Sometimes, that soulish mind of ours is the most difficult thing to bring into submission.

You can force the flesh to submit. You can fast, and with willpower, you can put yourself into extreme situations. But to control the soulish man is an entirely different thing!

Perhaps even now, as you are reading this, you are facing death in your mind, emotions, and will. You are having to let go of that intellectual way of thinking because the soulish man does not perceive the things of the Lord.

If you are to receive the pattern for His Church from the Spirit of God, you are not going to get it from your mind. You are going to get it from the Spirit. And to get it from the Spirit of God, you need to get into the Spirit.

To get into the Spirit, you need to put away all natural things. You need to put away your mind, put away your desires, and put away your intellectual thinking. You need to put away everything that you have been trying to figure out about this whole apostolic call up until now. It is time to get the truth. And you are only going to get the truth from the Spirit of God.

Face-to-Face With the Lord

In my personal experience, I believe that the most important aspect of climbing the mountain would be the face-to-face relationship with the Lord Jesus. This is a subject very close to my heart.

The most important and most magnificent miracle that is accomplished in you during this time is learning to speak with the

Lord face-to-face. You need to know Him as a friend, brother, father - as everything!

This is the most poignant thing that is going to be accomplished in your life. If you receive or learn nothing else on the mountain, may it be that you develop that face-to-face relationship with the Lord Jesus.

No matter how weak you are, or no matter how you fail and mess up, He will always be there to take you through and vindicate you. He will always be there to lift you up, encourage you, speak to you and give you the right direction, even when you miss it.

Getting the pattern is important. But without this face-to-face relationship, you will flounder in the dark and have nowhere to go. Without that face-to-face relationship, you will be constantly walking out of His will because you will not feel His heart. You need to come to a place where you feel His heart.

REACHING MATURITY: PERFECT LOVE

What does the face-to-face relationship accomplish in you? Most importantly, it accomplishes maturity.

You say,

"What! Are you kidding? I've been in ministry now for forty years."

"I'm fifty years old. I know what maturity is."

"I've been preaching for longer than you've been alive. Don't tell me I need to be mature."

Well, what is maturity? Does maturity mean you are gray? What does maturity mean? Does it mean you are old? Does it depend on how many years you have been saved?

> *1 Corinthians 13:11* When I was a child, I spoke as a child, I understood as a child, I thought as a child; but when I became a man, I put away childish things.

In other words, I grew up and became mature. What is Paul speaking about in this passage? You should know this chapter. It is the love chapter.

He was saying, "Yes, you can prophesy, and you can flow in the gifts. All these are good things. But until you have perfected love, you have nothing. Until you have a face-to-face relationship with the Lord Jesus Christ, you have not yet entered maturity."

THE POWER OF LOVE

The basis of maturity in the spiritual walk is not your age. It is not your gender, your height, your hair color, or your stature. It is the face-to-face relationship with the Lord Jesus Christ and the power of love.

> *How mature is the force of love in you? That will depend on your maturity.*

Until you are walking in the Spirit and constantly walking in love, in communion with the Lord, you are not there yet.

You know, there is something about walking in love that I have really come to know firsthand, and that is that you cannot just "do it." Let's be honest here. Who can love everybody all the time? There are days when even my kids stretch that limit.

The people I love even stretch that limit, and I have to grit my teeth and say, "Forgiveness, forgiveness! Lord… forgiveness! Forgiveness!"

You grit your teeth, and you think, "Oh man, I really want to give them a piece of my mind!"

It is not easy to love by choice alone. In fact, it is impossible to love as the Scriptures say. So then, what is the solution?

The only way to be able to walk in that love relationship is to walk with Jesus. When you are in that face-to-face relationship where you are walking with Him on a daily basis, you will be walking in His love. As you receive it, it will flow out of you naturally.

A Vision of His Love

The Lord gave me a beautiful personal experience in the Spirit of this once. He took me up to a beautiful bedchamber. This was our secret place - just Him and me. It was the most beautiful room I had ever seen! Everything was rich with gold, satin, and lace. It was magnificent! It was like being in a palace of your dreams.

He put me on this couch and cleaned my clothes. He gave me wine to drink and poured oil over my head, and I looked beautiful. (Of course, visions can lie. They can over exaggerate my good side... but it was my moment, so I reveled in it!)

I looked gorgeous! The oil shone from my face, and I glowed. A beautiful golden light shone in this room. It was perfect.

Then the Lord showed me what it looked like from outside the room. I saw that even though this was our secret place, there was darkness on the outside.

The darkness represented the natural world that we live in all the time. The secret place represented the realm of the Spirit.

While I was in the Spirit with the Lord Jesus, my clothes were beautiful and white, and I looked beautiful. Then, in my vision, I stepped out on my own, into the darkness of the world. I had not taken two or three steps, and my clothes looked soiled. My hair started looking dirty, and my face started losing its shine.

I saw what happened and thought, "Yuck!", and I ran back to the secret place again. I had not been in His presence long, and suddenly, the stains started fading. I was transformed again to that beautiful person.

Then the Lord Jesus changed it up again. He took my hand, and He led me out into the world again. However, this time He was walking with me, holding my hand. I noticed that, while He was holding my hand, the beautiful light that had been in the secret place went with us into the world.

My clothes also stayed bright. For as long as I held His hand, I remained in the same state as when I was alone with Him in the secret place.

Now that is what happens to a lot of us. We spend time with the Lord in His presence. But then, we go out into the world – we leave Him behind. We go out, and we become grubby, discouraged and depressed. We get shot down and do not walk in His love.

You see, it is not enough just to go to the Lord every now and again. You have to take Him with you. That is really what the mountain is all about. It is getting to the place where you can take the Lord Jesus with you wherever you go.

Taking the Time

For this kind of change to take place, you need to take longer than an hour – or even two or three hours a day. The time that the Lord allocates to you may be specific, but for me, it is usually for a time of about two weeks that the Lord will specifically say to me, "Set this time aside."

During this mountain experience, you will spend time in His presence on a daily basis - morning, noon, and night - continually soaking in His presence. You will let Him change you, teach you, and get through to you, because sometimes, the Lord is not finished talking yet after the hour is up, and we leave. We seem to cut Him short.

I have seen this even in a mentoring relationship. I have learned that when you live with somebody, your progress increases so much more rapidly than if you just see them one hour a week, or even one hour a day. But, when you live with them, you are changed at a much quicker rate.

The Lord wants you to move away from just spending isolated times with Him to actually committing a set time of living with Him on a continual basis. This is where you wake up with Him, go to sleep with Him, eat, talk, and joke with Him - even going to the bathroom with Him!

That is really what I am talking about. It is about being in the spiritual realm consistently, until you can come to the place where you can hear a pin drop - where you can hear His voice over the noise around you. It is so that when you walk out into the world, you can hear Him louder than you can hear everybody else yelling around you.

That is what the Lord is calling you to at this time, and it is going to be the most magnificent and beautiful time of your life! You are going to be that little bud that has been closed over, and you cannot see its beauty. By the time you come down from that mountain, you are going to have blossomed into something very beautiful. You see, you need to know as you are known.

> **1 Corinthians 13:12** *For now we see in a mirror, dimly, but then face to face. Now I know in part, but then I shall know just as I also am known.*

The Lord will become so real to you. He will be as another person. Does this not burn in your heart? Even as I share here, doesn't that passion burn in the pit of your stomach that you will give up food for it? Does it not burn so deeply in the pit of your stomach that you will give up your life for it?

That is what the Lord is asking of you. Would you let it burn so deeply right in the middle of you that you will do anything to have that face-to-face relationship? You know, the Lord is not asking you to be clever. He is not asking you to be anything special. He is asking you to passionately desire it!

He wants you to passionately desire Him as He passionately desires you. I want to tell you that the Lord Jesus is passionately in love with His Bride, and He is passionately in love with you. If you would just seek to passionately love Him in return, that is all He requires.

This is your starting point. It is your starting point of change, and of progress. It is also your starting point to your journey to apostolic office.

The call to the mountain draws you into apostolic training. It sustains you during it and adds to you once you are in office.

So, if you are at that point right now, where you have been vacillating and wondering which step to take next - this is it. You cannot come down from the mountain.

In fact, you cannot progress in your apostolic ministry until you have that kind of relationship with the Lord Jesus.

Moses could not come down from the mountain and say, "Thus saith the Lord," until he had heard Him.

Moses could not say, "The Lord says we must build a Tabernacle," until he had actually heard the Lord say it!

You cannot open your big mouth and give any great words of wisdom, until you have heard the Lord say so. You are not going to hear the Lord say so until you have gone into the spiritual realm. Not until you are in that face-to-face relationship with Him, and you know as you are known.

CHAPTER 08

RECEIVING THE PATTERN

Chapter 08 – Receiving The Pattern

After you have spent time in the Lord's presence, and He has become a real person to you, you are ready to begin receiving the pattern.

Do you know that Moses went up the mountain multiple times? (We will be looking at that in the next couple of chapters) It was only on the sixth trip that he received the pattern for the Tabernacle. In the past, I always imagined he went up there, cut his stones, and received the pattern. That is what you see in the movie "The Prince of Egypt", right? He just took a quick trip and got the tablets.

The Progression

It was not so. It was a progression. The first time Moses went up, the Lord gave him instructions on how the people were to sacrifice.

He said, "Now this is what I want them to do. I want them to worship me. I want them to perform burnt offerings."

The fourth time he went up, God actually gave Moses the Ten Commandments. They were not written, but He gave Moses the Ten Commandments verbally.

Moses went down, and he said to the people, "Here are the Ten Commandments, guys. This is what we have to do."

Then Moses went up in that glory cloud again, and the Lord gave him the pattern. That is when the tablets were carved with the Ten Commandments. You see, it was a progression. The Lord had to take the people through stages so that they could absorb it all. If He had given them everything all at once, it would have overwhelmed them.

He said, "Okay, let's begin first with how you should live. This is how I want you to sort your lives out now. Get in order. Sort out what needs to be done now. Then, these are the laws that you must live by."

After that, He gave them the pattern for the Tabernacle. He gave a pattern for praise and worship. Only then did He say, "Okay, now apply these laws."

In the same way, the Lord is going to take you through various stages.

Do not think, "Oh, I can't wait! I'm going to get into the presence of the Lord, and He's going to give me the pattern. Then, I'm going to zoom out of there and change the world …"

STEP 1: BROUGHT TO ORDER

Just calm yourself down and spend some time in His presence, waiting and listening. The chances are the first thing that is going to happen is you are going to be brought to order.

I know you do not want to hear that. I know you wanted to hear about the glory. We all like to hear about the glory. However, you are going to be brought to order first.

The Lord is going to say, "Okay, this relationship, habit, and personal desire… I want them out.

These are the doctrines I want changed.

Your ability to handle pressure needs to be adjusted.

That bitterness and that anger has to go! That selfishness and love for worldly things - it must go."

As you come into the Lord's presence, you could have things highlighted from your past. Your attitudes, and even your present life that needs to be brought to order, will stand out.

> *Before the Lord can give you the pattern, you need to be conditioned to receive it.*

A call to order is required because while you still have bitterness in your heart and preconceived ideas in your head, you cannot receive that pattern.

That is one very big reason why the Lord takes you up the mountain. It is to get you out of the system that you were in. He needs to pull you out of that status quo system and structure, so that you can actually perceive things as they are and see clearly.

While you are in it, your perception is fuzzy. You cannot see clearly. So the Lord has to pull you out of that, so you can look objectively and see exactly what is wrong with the system, and what you won't want to be part of.

STEP 2: SEEING THE PATTERN IN YOU

We all know that the commandments were written on tablets of stone. Everybody knows that.

As I came to the Lord, I had many questions. I said, "Lord, what about the pattern? Where is the pattern going to be? Where is it going to go? So, what is it going to look like? Come on Lord, tell us."

> **Hebrews 10:16** *"This is the covenant that I will make with them after those days, says the Lord: I will put My laws into their hearts, and in their minds I will write them,"*

It hit me right between the eyes. Do you know where the pattern is going to be written? It is going to be written inside of you. Are we not the temples of the Holy Spirit? Are we not the modern day temple of the Lord Jesus Christ?

Now, in the Old Testament, when the temple and the tabernacle had been completed, His glory came down.

Once the pattern for the Tabernacle is complete, the glory will come, just as it came on Moses after his sixth visit.

The tabernacle needs to be completed, and it needs to be completed in you. That is why you have been going through so much change.

The pattern of the Lord needs to be completed in your mind - in your attitude, in your conceptions, and in your way of seeing things. It needs to be firmly rooted in the foundation of your own heart.

This is why you have gone through so much preparation. It is because the Lord has to crack away everything that is not of Him, and everything that is not part of His pattern.

The apostolic pattern that the Lord has for you has to be grafted inside of you. You need to see with His eyes, feel with His heart, and act with His actions.

Before you can come down from the mountain and say, "Okay people, this is what it looks like," it has to be in you first. It has to be carved in the stone of your heart before you can show it to anybody else.

This is also one of the main reasons why you are called up to the mountain of God. It is so that the pattern can become alive and real in you.

> **The pattern must become more real to you than the food that you eat, the street that you walk on, or the people that you talk to.**

STEP 3: PERSONAL TRANSFIGURATION

You need to eat it and live it, breathe it, and know it with every fiber of your being. Once this has been accomplished, the glory of God is going to come down. When you come down from that mountain, the people are going to run because your face is going to be glowing with His glory!

That is what will happen to you. A transfiguration is going to occur, just like Jesus was transfigured - you will be changed. It will be like in the time where Peter, James, and John saw Jesus with Elijah and Moses. They were frightened of Him because of the way He looked. (Matt 16:28)

This is what the Lord is going to do with you. You are going to be transfigured, but it is going to begin from within.

The Lord is not going to say to you, "Okay, this is the structure of my Church."

He is going to say, "Here, let me carve the structure of my Church in your heart."

That is what is going to happen. It will happen by a change of attitude, passion, directions, and by your own templates being rearranged.

Change Begins With You

Why does the Lord set the bar so high for the apostle? Why doesn't He call every believer to this level of accountability?

It is because not everyone has what it takes to go through the trials. Not everyone has received the same dispensation of grace.

> **Ephesians 3:1** *For this reason I, Paul, the prisoner of Christ Jesus for you Gentiles—*
>
> *2 if indeed you have heard of the dispensation of the grace of God which was given to me for you,*

God, in His foresight, has given each of us a dispensation of grace. The apostle has been given a dispensation that requires more of him.

Apostles are handpicked. For the Lord to take every single Christian and change their templates would take too long. It is easier to pick out one man and rearrange his templates, put the fire in him, and then send that fire out to the rest.

So, if you are looking to the Lord to change the whole group that you are in, forget about it. It is not going to happen that way. It is going to happen with you first. Then, the fire you face and the change you experience will filter down to the others.

You want revival. You want the glory. You want the Church as you see it and know it to be in the Spirit. Then, know that it begins with you!

Stop saying, "Oh Lord, change my congregation. Change the people. They are a stubborn people! Lord, they are full of bitterness. Break their hearts of stone!"

No! Rather, it should read, "Lord, break my heart. Lord, I'm bitter. Lord, I'm selfish. I need change. Change me, Lord!"

Go and look in the mirror because that is where the Lord is going to put His glory first. Once you receive it, you will then be responsible before God to take the glory down to the people.

Moses did not cry out on the mountain and say, "Oh Lord, show the people your glory." He said, "Lord, I want to see your glory. I want to know your glory."

When he came down the mountain, they woke up pretty smartly. They got the fright of their lives! They dared not stand against Moses. They knew, "God is with this man."

That is how you are going to bring change. You are not going to bring change by pouring down judgment, hellfire, and brimstone on the people you minister to. The change is going to be borne from the change in your own heart.

> *If you really desire to see the body of Christ become the pattern that is in heaven, then you first need to carry that pattern in your heart. Then, you can minister it to everyone else.*

STEP 4: RECEIVING INSTRUCTIONS

Once you have received the pattern, that is the time the Lord will give you instructions on what to do with it. Moses had received the pattern and had received the second set of tablets (we will not go into that drama of when the Israelites worshipped the calf). It was at this time that the Lord gave him instructions on what to do with the pattern.

He said, "I'm going to give an angel to you, and he is going to go ahead of you. Go and build the tabernacle. The enemies will run ahead of you, but I am going to take good care of you. Do not worry about it." (Exodus 23)

It was only after he had received the pattern and the glory of the Lord, that God gave him the instruction and said, "Okay, Moses, now this is what you do with that pattern. This is how you apply what I've given you."

So, perhaps you are not quite receiving the exact instructions and direction from the Lord that you want right now. Perhaps you are becoming frustrated. If so, then you need to get back to these points.

Have you developed the face-to-face relationship? Are you walking in the maturity of love?

Have you received the pattern in your heart?

Do you have a very clear picture in your mind of what the body of Christ looks like?

Do you know what you want it to look like, what you want to accomplish, and what the Lord wants to accomplish?

Are your attitudes and emotions in accordance with the Word of God and the instruction He has given to you?

Qualifying for the Next Stage

If so, then the instructions will follow. If not, then you need to go and look back at the other steps and see where you are lacking. The Lord is not going to tell you how to apply what He has put in you, unless your heart is in the right place.

He is not going to give somebody a tool to cut diamonds when that person doesn't have a clue how to cut them.

You cannot just take any guy off the street and say, "Hey, do you mind cutting this diamond for me?"

He will end up smashing the beautiful, expensive diamond to bits and ruining it. You need to know what you are doing. You need to wield the correct tools and apply the correct pressure.

Until you have learned these things and know them, the Lord is not going to give you instructions and release you into the body of Christ. If He did, you would go around with a chisel, smashing diamonds everywhere.

You are supposed to be perfecting the Church, not ruining it. It is an immense responsibility that we carry as apostles, and it needs to be seen as such.

This is not a title. This is a responsibility.

If I were you, I would not be shouting my mouth off too much and saying, "I'm a great apostle of God," because, in reality, it is a demotion.

It means a position of death and humbling, of washing dirty, stinky feet! That is what being an apostle is about. So, do not go around carrying that title as though you have big stripes on your shoulders, like in the army.

This is not for the world to see. If you want to go carrying around that big title, and you make a mistake, then you will see the wrath of that title.

Do not go around wielding instruments that you do not know how to use yet. Do not go around crushing diamonds that you do not know how to cut correctly. You also cannot go around trying to put a pattern into existence that you have not yet received.

God was pretty specific with Moses. He said, "Make it exactly according to my instructions! Not one inch out, or one inch in. Do it exactly like I told you."

The Right Attitudes

Before the Lord will give you instructions and release you, you had better have a very clear picture of where you are going.

Your attitude had also better be right before God. Your attitude must be one of humility, love, and servitude. It must not be one of arrogance, pride, and self-exaltation. If that is one thing that I get through to you in this book, it is that. Apostleship is a position of humility and of being on your face before God.

Your models are Moses and Jesus - they remained on their faces before the Father. Jesus was prepared to wash the feet of His disciples. If you are like that, in the days that come when people stand in opposition to you, like Korah did to Moses, they will not stand a chance. They will lose because the Lord will vindicate you!

He will be the one to stand in your stead, to wipe out and bring correction to those who stand against you. It is not your place to go vindicate yourself. It is your place to be in a face-to-face relationship with the Lord. You need to be as He is, speak as He speaks, and love as He loves.

Your Place

You have not been brought to this world to judge it, or brought to the body of Christ to judge it. You have been called to the body of Christ to make it a city set on a hill that shines to every nation so that they are drawn to it by its glory.

You are not there to smash it or trample it underfoot. You are not there to slay the innocent lambs. You are there to make the body of Christ so beautiful that every nation in this world will be clamoring for her attention!

I look at when the people of Israel left Egypt and how it says that a mixed multitude went with them. They took one look at the Israelites and said, "Pharaoh's side or Moses' side? Forget it -

Moses is more blessed! We're going with him. I'm not sticking with these losers."

That is what we need to be accomplishing in the body of Christ. We need to make a city that is set on a hill that is beautiful to behold that everybody will flock to it.

That is what we are accomplishing. We are building up and putting the pieces together for God's perfect Church. The Lord is going to give you a piece and me a piece. He is going to give each apostle a piece, and we are going to bring it together and make the body of Christ into something spectacular!

But, we cannot put those pieces together until the pieces are within us. We need to be shaped, and we need to be changed in our hearts. You will be shaped, and you will be changed. When you are, that is when the Lord is going to give you the pattern.

CHAPTER 09

IMPARTING THE FIRE

Chapter 09 – Imparting the Fire

You have received the instructions. You have spent time with the Lord and developed that face-to-face relationship. You have spent much time walking in the Spirit and spending your time in the spiritual realm.

Now comes a time when you will have to walk out into the world, just like I shared in my vision in a previous chapter. The time of being on top of the mountain is about to end.

It is time to bring the mountain down to God's people.

This time though, you will not walk out alone, or in the flesh. You walk out with the Lord holding your hand. When you do that, you take the mountain, and the glory of God with you.

That is the whole point of your mountain experience, because you cannot bring change to the body of Christ until you come down from that mountain.

How does a fire spread? It doesn't fall on the ground out of the sky and burn down an entire forest.

It starts with one tree. In fact, it can start with one little bush and spread from there. Before you know it, the whole forest is ablaze.

You are just that little bush. Get yourself on fire. Get yourself filled with the glory of the Lord. Then come down with that fire. Do not snuff it out before you make it down. Bring it with you and take it to the people.

Spread the Fire

You know, when Moses had come down and had built the tabernacle, it says he came out, and he blessed the people. He and Joshua blessed the people and imparted the blessing and promises of the Lord.

The Lord said, "I will make you a nation. You will be the head and not the tail, above only and not beneath. You will always be victorious, and your enemies will run before you!" (Deuteronomy 28)

They blessed the people and imparted that blessing and the promises of God to them.

Didn't Jesus do the same? After all, the disciples had come together. Their hearts had been changed, and they stood at Pentecost - what happened? The fire came down. The first time Jesus saw them after He had resurrected, what did He say? The Scriptures say He breathed into them and said, "Receive the Holy Spirit. Here it is." (John 20:22)

You see, Jesus had gone to the ultimate mountain! He had gone to the mountain of the Lord in the heavenly realm. You do not get it any better than that!

He came down and said to His disciples, "Okay guys, I've got the blessing. Receive it!", and He imparted it to them.

We know what happened at Pentecost. As important as it is to receive the glory of the Lord on the mountain, it is just as vital to bring that glory down to the people and impart it to them.

ONE AT A TIME

Perhaps you will tell me, "Well, I can't really do that because I'm not in the position where I have a congregation."

"You know, I've just got a couple of people. I'm not really in active ministry at the moment."

There are no excuses because the body of Christ has many members. All you need to do is find one person. If that is all the Lord has called you to, take one person at a time that you can impart to. Impart that change, that breath of life, and that promise. Impart the fire and blessing, and stir up their spirit and their heart.

Shatter those blinds that are over their eyes and ears that are stopping them from seeing, hearing, and speaking. If you can take one person and breathe the life that you have received into them and see them come to life, then you have accomplished your purpose.

Stop thinking in big numbers. Stop thinking "fame and recognition." Think, "body of Christ." Think, "individual people." Each of us are stones making up the temple of the Lord. Each of us are members of one body in Christ.

Grab a member - any member. Take somebody who is unsaved. Make him a member, and breathe the life into him. Start with the person that is with you. If you are married, take your husband or wife. Take your children, your grandparents or relatives. Take whoever is near you, and breathe the life of the Lord into them. Get their spirits going.

Take what the Lord has given to you, and breathe it into just one person. As they get on fire, they will light somebody else, in turn. I want to tell you, before long, you will have a forest fire that will be seen for miles!

A lot of the time, what happens is that you are motivated by your experience with God. You are excited about the revelation God has given to you.

Then you go to everyone and say, "Guys, look what the Lord has done. Come on, let's go!"

They take one look at you and say, "Well, why should we? I don't feel like it."

What happens then is that fire and glory that the Lord has imparted to you get squelched. You are de-motivated.

> ***The solution? Do not bite off more than you can chew. Let's be practical. Start with one person.***

Then, move on to imparting to two people and three people, and it will grow from there.

Hey, Jesus only took twelve. He may have preached to the multitudes, but He only breathed that kind of impartation into twelve. So, do not think that you need to go to the thousands.

STARTING A REVIVAL

Start with the person who is closest to you, particularly if it is your spouse. That is the most important. Take your husband, take your wife. Breathe that into them. Impart it into them. Shake them and change them.

Get a fire starting in their belly. Let them catch the vision with you. Then, the two of you can stand together, and you have double power. Then, grab somebody else, and somebody else.

I was reading about the Azusa Street revival and how this is exactly what happened with Seymour. They had a little house gathering. He just had his family around. They didn't even have anything magnificent. He did not even have a church.

They were just getting together in a home with the people he knew - his close relatives. Before you knew it, their home was too small. Before you knew it... they had the Azusa Street revival, where people from all over the world were coming to get a touch!

You see, he was not so grand and ambitious as to say, "That was a great meeting. We're making an announcement. Great Apostle Seymour is going to be in town this week. Everybody, bring your friends, bring your checkbooks..."

No, he got his friends and his close family together, and he went on a fast. They just got together and sat in the lounge, and the power came down.

That is where it is going to happen in your life too. It is not going to happen with the big crowds. It is not going to happen in front of multitudes. It is going to happen in your heart, in your home, in your community, and in your state. Then, it is going to spread like wildfire all over the world. Start where you are at. It is good to have a big vision. But, be practical and start where you are at with those closest to you.

You know, so often, I see people overextending themselves for others, but they are neglecting their families. Their vision consumes them "out there" instead of them realizing that the power starts "in here."

If you would just pour into your family, using the fire that is inside of you, you would have them standing with you. You would have backup that would surpass none that anybody else could give you.

APOSTOLIC TEAMS

This is really what I believe the Lord is creating in these end-times. He is raising up apostolic teams. Families – husbands, wives, and children coming together as teams.

This is where the power is going to be. You need to receive that pattern, that mandate, that change and face-to-face relationship on behalf of your family. Then, once you have it, you need to impart it to them.

Once you have imparted it to them, trust me, it is going to start spreading. It is going to start changing lives. You will be very actively involved in apostolic office.

Apostolic office does not mean standing in front of thousands of people. It means laying a foundation. Whether you are laying that foundation in the heart of one person, or laying it in the hearts of ten thousand people, you are still laying a foundation.

And you are no less an apostle than one who is laying the foundation in tens of thousands. You are no less because you are doing His work and His will.

PRAYER

As you have read the last 3 chapters, I know that I have probably stirred up a lot of things in you. Even in the Spirit now, I sense a churning of many things. I sense a churning of excitement, and perhaps of a desire to move into that face-to-face relationship with the Lord Jesus. I sense also a frustration of not being able to break through that barrier to move into that relationship.

I would just like to pray with you, that the Lord would intervene and come into your life right now and into your heart. I pray that He would breathe that life right into you that would open your eyes to His presence, to His love, and to His affection for you, that you may now start moving to the fullness of your calling.

> *Father, I come before you humbly right now. Jesus, I submit myself to you, and I pray on behalf of your people. Father, their hearts are dry. Their hearts are empty. Jesus, your apostles need you. They need to see you face-to-face. They need to know you in a more real way than they know themselves. Oh Father, how your heart burns for each one of them!*
>
> *Come, Holy Spirit, and breathe into the hearts of your apostles right now. Breathe into them and break down every barrier. Break down every bitterness and every fear. Breathe into their lives right now and raise them up wherever they stand.*
>
> *Satan, I stand against you right now in the name of Jesus. I come against every lie. I come against every word of condemnation, guilt, and fear. I bind you in Jesus' name, and you will loose your hands right now off these servants of God whom you have bound with your accusation and condemnation!*
>
> *I shatter those shells over your mind. I shatter those shells over your heart in the name of Jesus. I send a sword forth that would divide even to the spirit and soul right now.*

May it cut away everything that is preventing the face-to-face love relationship in the name of Jesus. Jesus, pour in your love right now. The Lord is with you right now.

Thank you, Holy Spirit. Your will be done on earth as it is in Heaven. In Jesus' name. Amen.

CHAPTER 10

THE 7 MOUNTAIN TOP EXPERIENCES

Chapter 10 – The 7 Mountain Top Experiences

We begin this chapter with Moses having just had his burning bush experience, and the Lord is busy speaking to him.

> *Exodus 3:12* So He said, "I will certainly be with you. And this shall be a sign to you that I have sent you: When you have brought the people out of Egypt, you shall serve God on this mountain."

The angel was speaking about Mount Sinai. He was speaking about Moses when he first came and saw the burning bush and had an encounter with God. God gave him his mandate to go and get the children of Israel and take them to the Promised Land.

The Lord said to him at that time, "This is a sign that I am going to give you that you will return to this mountain. You are going to bring my people back to this very place where you had your encounter with me, Moses. You will bring them where you experienced me for the first time and started getting an inkling of what I have called you to do. You are coming back."

A Broad Picture

I already covered in, "Climbing the Mountain", how you need to climb the mountain to receive that mandate from the Lord, how you need to go and seek His face and get a direction, a vision, and a confirmation of where you are heading in your apostolic calling.

But, it is not a once-off event. In fact, your first climb up the mountain is really only the beginning. The first climb is when you start to realize, "Hey, there's something more to this. There's a greater call and purpose."

You stop wandering around aimlessly in the wilderness, and you start getting a direction and a vision. All the Lord told Moses was, "Go there to Egypt. Go and get my people out."

Moses said, "How? When? Why? How much? How am I going to do it? What am I going to say?"

The Lord said, "Just go there. I'll give you the words."

So, he went with a broad picture of what he was called to do. He knew, "Okay, I'm going to take the children of Israel, get them away from Pharaoh, and take them to the Promised Land."

That is all the Lord told Moses to do. He gave him a couple of signs and sent him on his way. But as to how he was going to accomplish this, as to how he would lead the children of Israel and what route he was going to take, Moses didn't have a clue!

This is where this chapter will pick up. We will begin with you having had an experience with the Lord. You have received your mandate. You know the broad picture. You have a general idea in your heart of where you are going to go and what you are going to do. However, as to the fine details and how to actually carry out that mandate, it is still a secret to you.

That is why you must return to the mountain. You must return for a number of reasons. As we go through each one in the chapters that follow, and share each visit to the mountain, realize that through your apostolic walk, you will continue climbing the mountain. It is not something you do just once.

It is not something that you say, "Well, I climbed the mountain yesterday, and now it's over."

> *"Climbing the mountain" for an apostle is a continual state of being in the presence of the Father.*

MANY VISITS

Your apostolic call begins and ends on the mountain. The very last time Moses ever climbed the mountain was to be with the Lord. You will climb the mountain continually through your apostolic walk until you have completed the mandate that the Lord has given you.

You have received the mandate. You will then be empowered to complete the mandate. You will be changed from image to image, from glory to glory. You may start off as a little weak Moses in the backside of the desert. You may not be able to speak. You stutter and stammer and are too afraid to head out into the big mean system.

By the end of this journey, we see Moses leading the whole nation of Israel into war and starting to take the land for God. A change had come.

What is the purpose of returning to the mountain? Why do you have to go back? You go back so that you can enter into the glory of the Father. Sure, you had an experience with the Holy Spirit. Sure, the power came down, and you received your revelation and your mandate. But, that is not good enough. You see, that experience is not going to carry you through the journey.

That experience is like a transition. It is one little moment. It is one picture. Sure, it gave you hope. It gave you faith, and it gave you love. Yet, that fire will not carry you through the whole journey because you are going to face hard times.

You will face obstacles, and you need something more substantial than just zeal, fire, or vision. You need a relationship with the Father!

Zeal is not enough. Vision is not enough. Potential is not enough. Not even commitment is enough! To get you through this journey, you need a face-to-face relationship with the Father because it is by His strength, power, and authority that you are going to lead the church of God into victory.

Your zeal is not going to cut it, nor will your ability cut it. It is not your great commitment and your great sacrifice that is going to cut it. It is His anointing and His power and authority that is going to take you through.

His Chosen Vessel

It is not just about you anymore. Now, Moses is leading the children of Israel! You see you are called to death. You are called to change, and in yourself, you are changed. You, in yourself, are taken from image to image, and that is good. As you have laid your life down, the Lord has changed and molded you, and that is wonderful.

You have been made into a vessel, but you're an empty vessel. You may have been made by the hands of the Master, you may be spectacular to look at, and you may have a magnificent use. You may be the most useful vessel in the house, but until you contain the essence of the Father, you are nothing but empty!

You may look and sound good, but until you are filled with the glory of the Father so that He is brimming from you, people's lives will not change. The children of God will not be taken to the Promised Land.

Reflecting His Glory

Up until now, all the preparation and training has been training you, shaping you, and making you into that vessel fit for His glory. Now it is time you are filled with His glory, emanate His glory, and stand in His glory - that when man looks at you, they do not see the vessel, but they see His glory.

Up until now, you have been created into a vessel that is fit to hold that glory. You have qualified. Through all this hell you have been through, and all these tough times, congratulations! You have only now just qualified to go through the hardest part. You have only now qualified to actually take into yourself some of that glory and some of that anointing.

Now the real work begins! Now as you have been built up, you will disappear in His cloud, and all that they will see will be God, and Him alone. They will not see you, your ability, your deaths or even the price you had to pay.

They will not see your great humility. They will not see any of the great characteristics that you have built and died for. They will see His glory - and that is the reward of the apostle. I cannot think of any greater reward than to go through all of that preparation and training than to stand and reflect the glory of the Father.

You start off as an imperfect vessel. By the end of this journey, you will be reflecting the glory of the Father. You will go up the mountain in fear and trembling, as you see the lightning and thunder, and as you hear the trumpets sound.

You will think, "Oh Lord, how can I go up there? How could I come face-to-face with the Father in my sin, in my weakness, and in my inability?"

You will come down in power though. You will come down in the authority of the Father, and with the awe of His presence on you.

> *You will go up in trembling and you will come down in glory. You will go up in fear and come down in boldness. You will be changed from glory to glory with each step you take and each time you climb.*

I shared in, "Climbing the Mountain", that you had to leave everything behind you before you could climb the mountain. So now, we are going to look at the transition you take with each different step, and each stage, and the transformation that takes place with each visit.

THE 1ST VISIT: THE PROMISE

> ***Exodus 19:3** And Moses went up to God, and the Lord called to him from the mountain, saying, "Thus you shall say to the house of Jacob, and tell the children of Israel:*
>
> *4 "You have seen what I did to the Egyptians, and how I bore you on eagles' wings and brought you to Myself.*

> *5 Now therefore, if you will indeed obey My voice and keep My covenant, then you shall be a special treasure to Me above all people; for all the earth is Mine.*
>
> *6 And you shall be to Me a kingdom of priests and a holy nation.' These are the words which you shall speak to the children of Israel."*

What is your first visit to the mountain? Let's take a look at Moses.

God called to him from the mountaintop. The children of Israel had finally returned to Mount Sinai and had gathered there. They had gone through everything, and now about three months after they had left Egypt, they came to the mountain.

This is the sign that God spoke of to Moses at the very beginning. Three months later, he was back at the mountain, and the children of Israel were with him. God called to him from the mountain and said, "Moses come up."

So, he went up to meet God on the mountain, and it was here that God said to him, "I am going to establish Israel."

At the burning bush, He gave Moses a tremendous promise of how He was going to lead them to a land of milk and honey. He told Moses how He was going to make the nations bow before them.

Now, God promises how He will make them a light to the nations as they obey His ordinances, submit to Him, and follow His command. They will rise up in authority and power.

This is the first visit. You will be called to the mountain. There will be a time in your apostolic walk where you will receive that call. You will hear God's voice from the mountain saying, "Now is the time. Come up the mountain."

This may come to you in various ways. You may receive a prophetic word. You may see it in the Scriptures. It may be a personal revelation. Somebody might feel led to share it with you, but it will be a personal conviction.

In my case, I felt a drawing, a sudden quieting down of everything around me and of being somewhere else. It felt like I was not being involved in daily activities and was being taken away.

It is almost as if I was in another world, and I felt that nudging that said, "Come away. Come away from everything! Put away your responsibilities. Put away your cares. Put away your needs and your concerns. Come away. It's time to climb the mountain. It's time to experience the Father."

INTRODUCTION TO THE FATHER

The first few times you go, it is an introduction. There is nothing deep and intense about it. The Lord will start sharing His heart with you. He will give you a promise for His people. He will start giving you a picture of what will take place and of what He desires to do through you and with you.

So, the first visit is really just a taste of what is to come. Already in that first visit, you will start getting a feel of who the Father is, of what to expect, and you will start feeling a change coming in yourself.

Suddenly, everything will start melting off you. All the cares and all the little nit-picky things that you are always worried about won't matter anymore. When you are standing in the presence of Almighty God who has this whole world as His footstool, what the kids are doing just doesn't seem to matter. What you have to cook for dinner is really quite insignificant.

The prophet over there who is speaking against your ministry just doesn't matter anymore. The pastor over there that is standing up and warning his congregation about you just doesn't matter anymore, because in the presence of an awesome God - these things fall away.

You will start experiencing a change that leaves you saying, "That really doesn't bother me anymore, and really it is insignificant. It doesn't matter!"

You will begin to know... that you know - that God is in control, because you will begin receiving a revelation of who He really is. You see, it is one thing to know of God, but it is another thing to really know God.

It is just like when Joshua said, "Up until now I knew of you, but now I have seen you, and I know you," and he trembled in the face of the Father.

He knew who God was, and he said, "Who am I that you have done all these magnificent things?"

Then he went through all the animals and how magnificent they are, and how God in His might had created all these things. The penny started dropping. When you look at the grand scheme of things, all these other things pass away. They fade, and the maturity starts coming out.

A security starts coming because you realize that your ministry, and the security of your ministry, does not lie in you. It lies in the hands of the Father. When you can see and experience the Father for the first time, you start getting His confidence because you know, *"Greater is He that is me, than he that is in the world."*

You don't just know it mentally anymore. You know it in your heart. You feel it, and it becomes part of you. When that starts happening, you have started entering into a relationship with the Father because it begins to consume you. You start to absorb it, and you start to be it. That is just the introduction.

THE 2ND VISIT: MAKING A CONTRACT WITH GOD

> ***Exodus 19:8*** *Then all the people answered together and said, "All that the Lord has spoken we will do." So Moses brought back the words of the people to the Lord.*
>
> *9 And the Lord said to Moses,* **"Behold, I come to you in the thick cloud, that the people may hear when I speak with you, and believe you forever."**
>
> *So Moses told the words of the people to the Lord.*

> *10 Then the Lord said to Moses, "Go to the people and consecrate them today and tomorrow, and let them wash their clothes.*
>
> *11 And let them be ready for the third day. For on the third day the Lord will come down upon Mount Sinai in the sight of all the people*

Now, there was the second visit. Moses had returned to the people, and he had said, "Listen guys, this is what God said. If we'll submit to Him, He will give us His promises."

They said, "That sounds great Moses. Go, and tell God we say okay." The message was to prepare themselves for something new to come.

The Lord did not just bring sudden change. He led them a step at a time. He told them how to prepare. Not every direction the Lord gives us is to "build" or to "do." Rather, in the second visit, the message was to wait on Him!

To prepare, wait, and be ready for Him to show up. So often, we want to force the direction God has. We want to force His promises and forget that they are on our terms. The greatest message at times can be found in the second visit, and it is, "Cleanse yourself, be ready, and wait!"

The Lord waits for you to commit to the call He has on your life. He does not simply throw it at you and force you to walk in it whether you like it or not!

We overlook this vital ascend so much! Just because you have a call does not mean you will automatically fulfill it!

No, this is two-sided. God gives the promise, and you put your own signature on the dotted line! You might have had your burning bush experience where you first received your call. You also might have received the promise of what He desires to do in your ministry and what He desires to do in His Church. However, there is something else that is vitally needed here.

Your commitment! The Scriptures tell us that Noah condemned the world when he built the ark. The day he picked up the first hammer and committed to the instruction, he gave God license in this earth.

Up until now, all you have is God's intention. If you want to be part of His active plan in the earth, you need to put yourself in a position to pay the price and to fulfill that call!

Even amongst the great manifestation of Father God on top of that mountain, not a single word of direction came until Moses could say, "Yes, Lord! The people and I commit and agree to your statutes. We will do this your way. We want the promise, and we are prepared to pay the price for it."

Have you experienced this climb up the mountain yet? Where are you in your journey? Have you had your burning bush experience? Have you received your promise? Then, God is waiting for you to step out in obedience and to commit. When you do that, you can be sure that the mountain will shake, and from this moment, you pass the point of no return.

Wait for it, because thunder and lighting are about to strike...

THE 3RD VISIT: CONFIRMATION OF YOUR CALL

> ***Exodus 19:24*** *Then the Lord said to him, "Away! Get down and then come up, you and Aaron with you. But do not let the priests and the people break through to come up to the Lord, lest He break out against them."*
>
> *25 So Moses went down to the people and spoke to them.*

Moses returned for his third climb with a conviction, "Yes! We are going to do this God's way!" However, before God got onto the good stuff, He answered Moses and His people with a profound confirmation.

During his second visit, the Lord gave Moses a promise in addition to the instruction for the people to prepare themselves. That promise was, "Tomorrow Moses, I am going to confirm your call in the face of the people."

The first time he went up, the Lord gave a promise for the people. The next time he went up, God gave a promise to Moses.

He said, "I'm going to descend on this mountain in my glory, Moses. Every eye will see it, and every single Israelite down there will look up and see my glory and hear me speaking from this cloud.

"They will know that I have placed my calling on you and that I have placed my authority and glory on you, Moses. They will know without a shadow of a doubt that God is here, that the Father has come down, and that I have appointed you."

Your Call Confirmed to Others

Up until now, you may know you have a call.

You say to people, "I'm called to be an apostle."

They say, "That's nice…", but they really don't believe you.

There will come a time when the Lord will confirm the call on your ministry. You will not need to confirm your calling. You will not need to stand up and beat people over the head because God will confirm your call. The glory of God will come down, and the Father will manifest Himself in you. It will confirm your calling, and they will know that the power of God is on you.

So, on that second visit, Moses went down the mountain again and said to the people, "Sanctify yourselves, for in three days God is going to appear to us."

They sanctified themselves, and three days later, there descended on Sinai a cloud, smoke, thunder and lightning. A trumpet blast went out summoning Moses up the mountain, and the people quaked in fear and terror because the whole mountain was shaking with the glory of God!

On his third visit, Moses was the bravest of them all as he ascended into a cloud of fire! If ever his office was proven, it was as his foot took the first step on that climb. God fulfilled His promises – His call on Moses was confirmed.

And so, the people, for the first time, met God, the Father, as they looked up the mountain and saw the cloud, and they feared. But, they knew that Moses had been called, and Moses began his journey.

His calling confirmed, the Lord took it a step further and had him tell the people again to obey His command. It is an interesting transition, this one, because you have so many different kinds of leaders.

You have those that are so quick to wear the title and boast of their gifts and abilities, but for those with a true apostolic call, it takes you some time to truly come to terms with the call.

The Greater Confirmation...

Perhaps the most profound aspect of this experience is not how much the call is confirmed to others as much as it is confirmed to you. To get the conviction that you are called to lead and to build.

I personally was most comfortable hiding behind other leaders. I was comfortable hiding behind my father and then comfortable hiding behind my husband. The responsibility and affront you get from "being up front" is no joke at all. I had too many insecurities and fears.

I feared failure. I feared man. I feared deception, and I feared that I could surely lead everyone down a garden path and destroy us all. (Yeah, the Lord had to deal with how much faith I had in myself instead of Him. Keep in mind, though, that we are just on our second mountain visit... there are a few more to go yet!)

And so, I remember struggling with God, asking Him why He kept giving the revelations to me instead of to my husband. The Lord came with lightning and thunder, "Do not tell me who to choose and what vessel I should pick up and pour out of! Did I not make your mouth? Did I not choose to use you? Will you tell me who I can and cannot use?"

Question answered. God is God, and He will pick up whom He pleases and anoint whom He pleases. This experience was life-changing for me. I came down from that experience, not just with a conviction of my call, but with a real sense of responsibility.

Someone had to keep climbing. Someone had to bring the message from God. Someone had to get the pattern and make sure it was built correctly. Most of all, the reality that struck me most was, that "someone"... was me!

I could no longer hide away. Instead, I had to be bold and climb up, time and again, until God had given us everything we needed to build as a ministry.

More to Come

Now, it would be wonderful to stay up the mountain forever. However, in reality, you have a ministry to take care of!

Right now, you have a pattern to keep establishing. This is why you visit the mountain time and again in various seasons. Once God has made His point, the time will come to return and "take care of business" and to ensure that everyone is following the pattern God has given. In the same way, Moses returned to make sure everyone was taking care of God's instruction because during his next visit, something epic would happen.

He would receive the Ten Commandments.

CHAPTER 11

4ᵀᴴ Visit: Your Ten Commandments

Chapter 11 – 4TH Visit: Your Ten Commandments

Now, we are starting to get a bit of an expansion on the mandate. Up until now, Moses really just figured that all he was called to do was take the children of Israel and lead them to the Promised Land. The Lord had a greater and deeper plan that was more detailed than what Moses realized.

I really don't think Moses thought that he was going to lay down the law for all the generations to come when he was sitting in the backside of the desert looking after some sheep. I don't think he felt very qualified.

Even now, perhaps he thought, "Well, my job's nearly over. I mean the land of milk and honey is just over the way there. Then, I can wash my hands of this and get back to the sheep farm."

Little did Moses know! Isn't that so the apostolic calling? You head out in a direction, and a lot of the time the Lord says, "Just head out. This is the general picture. This is the landscape and pretty much where you are going to go. I'll tell you the rest along the way. Just get moving."

Then slowly the puzzle, and the picture, unfolds.

How many people say, "I want the whole vision! Before I step out, I must have the whole picture, and I must have everything in place so that I know exactly where I am going."

It doesn't happen that way because the plan of God is multi-layered, and you need to understand each piece, and each layer, as you experience it. If the Lord had to give you the whole picture at one time, you wouldn't be able in your mind to retain it. You would certainly also not be ready to accept it, move with it, and function in it.

There needs to come some training. Each stage is a training period, and as you qualify, the Lord will give you another piece. Then, you will go through a little bit more training, you will qualify, and He will give you another piece, until you start building on it bit by bit, and until the building starts rising up.

ORGANIZATION AND ORDINANCE

The Lord showed us a vision that really illustrates this principle so well. He had given us the mandate and said, "I want you to lay a foundation for the fivefold ministry. I want you to go out there and begin laying a foundation for the body of Christ and the fivefold ministry."

We thought, "That sounds pretty good. We'll just get out there and start preaching."

That was the only direction the Lord gave us.

We needed more. Should we start with the prophets or with the teachers? What should our focus be? Yet, when we asked the Lord to give the rest of the steps, He said, "No. This is like building a house. You do not build one room of a house, then go and do the other room of the house and then another room. No, you lay the foundation. Then, you build all the rooms simultaneously piece by piece, and the whole house rises up until the whole house is complete."

We lived this vision very practically. The Lord would give us a piece of one room and then give us a piece of another room. He would give us a piece of the prophetic, a piece of the evangelistic, and then a piece of the apostolic. Then would come a piece of the pastoral and a piece of the teaching, and slowly, the training grew, one brick at a time.

At first, it didn't look like very much of anything. If you have ever been to a building site when they first begin building, you can't imagine what it will look like when it's finished. In fact, you think, "Is this big enough? Will this fit all the furniture in it? Is this straight enough? It doesn't make sense."

You think, "Where do the windows go? That wall looks too high."

With it being half finished, it doesn't look much like a building at all, but you continue putting one brick on top of another. And so, we continued putting one brick on top of the other until one day we looked up in the Spirit and were surprised at what we saw. We started seeing what this house was going to look like.

We realized, "Hey, we're nearly finished! This is where the kitchen goes. This is where the bathroom goes. This is where the bedroom is. And, this is where the dining hall is."

Slowly, it started taking shape. Now instead of having one room that was built, we had a whole house standing! Sure, it took longer. We were left in the dark for longer. We didn't see it take shape for longer. However, when it was built, it stood firm. It stood in its unity and in its wholeness. You could look at it, and it was solid because all the rooms were interlinked. All of them overlapped and joined up in just the right places.

You see, you start getting one little hobby horse, as we call it, or one little pet doctrine that you are always harping on. That would be like the children of Israel going on and on about, "The land of milk and honey. The land of milk and honey. All we want to do is take people to the land of milk and honey."

The Lord says, "I've got a couple of commandments for you."

"No. We want the land of milk and honey!"

It is not good enough to just have one room. You need to have a whole house. This is what God started doing with Moses as He began taking him up the mountain.

He said, "Okay sure, I want to lead you to a land of milk and honey. That is your destination. However, I am giving you a structure to set up when you get there. I'm giving you the Ten Commandments to start with. Then there's another room… I'm giving you the Law."

The Lord started giving Moses the pieces, one at a time, to start putting together the bigger picture.

The 4ᵗʰ Visit: The Ten Commandments

The Ten Commandments

c And God spoke all these words, saying:

2 "I am the Lord your God, who brought you out of the land of Egypt, out of the house of bondage.

3 "You shall have no other gods before Me.

4 "You shall not make for yourself a carved image—any likeness of anything that is in heaven above, or that is in the earth beneath, or that is in the water under the earth;

5 you shall not bow down to them nor serve them. For I, the Lord your God, am a jealous God, visiting the iniquity of the fathers upon the children to the third and fourth generations of those who hate Me, 6 but showing mercy to thousands, to those who love Me and keep My commandments.

7 "You shall not take the name of the Lord your God in vain, for the Lord will not hold him guiltless who takes His name in vain.

8 "Remember the Sabbath day, to keep it holy.

9 Six days you shall labor and do all your work, 10 but the seventh day is the Sabbath of the Lord your God. In it you shall do no work: you, nor your son, nor your daughter, nor your male servant, nor your female servant, nor your cattle, nor your stranger who is within your gates. 11 For in six days the Lord made the heavens and the earth, the sea, and all that is in them, and rested the seventh day. Therefore the Lord blessed the Sabbath day and hallowed it.

12 "Honor your father and your mother, that your days may be long upon the land which the Lord your God is giving you.

13 "You shall not murder.

14 "You shall not commit adultery.

> 15 "You shall not steal.
>
> 16 "You shall not bear false witness against your neighbor.
>
> 17 "You shall not covet your neighbor's house; you shall not covet your neighbor's wife, nor his male servant, nor his female servant, nor his ox, nor his donkey, nor anything that is your neighbor's."
>
> Exodus 20: 20 And Moses said to the people, "Do not fear; for God has come to test you, and that His fear may be before you, so that you may not sin." 21 So the people stood afar off, but Moses drew near the thick darkness where God was.
>
> 22 Then the Lord said to Moses, "Thus you shall say to the children of Israel: 'You have seen that I have talked with you from heaven. 23 You shall not make anything to be with Me—gods of silver or gods of gold you shall not make for yourselves.

Now comes the fourth visit. The third visit was when Moses went up with the lightning and the thunder.

On the fourth visit, he went up again, and the Lord gave him the Ten Commandments and ordinances for sacrifice. Here also, the Lord gave him the details of the Law.

THE TEN COMMANDMENTS

From this moment onward, the picture starts to come together. Not only does the Lord confirm Moses's call in the sight of everyone, but He begins giving a broad structure.

As you set out on your ministry, you were full of ambition, and you headed out where angels feared to tread! However, after a while, you started to realize something, "You needed structure and principles!"

I think this is even more relevant for those who moved from the prophetic to the apostolic. Prophets are notorious for their hunger to break down religious boundaries and to smash all sacred cows in sight! Ah yes... what would the Church be with the fire the prophets bring? I remember meeting one such prophet. Full of fire - his vision was to see all established church structure be torn down, and for believers to just follow the Spirit and just "go where God leads."

Sounds like freedom, doesn't it? However, if you have been along the road a little while, you come to realize that you need some principles for all that fire and Godly ambition. You need a vehicle to release all that anointing through. Yes... you need structure!

And so, as you begin to bring the pattern together, the Lord will begin with a general outline - principles and precepts that will make up the core foundation of your call.

There are many things that will change as you establish your mandate as an apostle. The Lord will shift you from mandate to mandate. He will have you reach out to every kind of person. Your vision will change constantly.

However, there is something that will never change, and those are your "Ten Commandments" that you receive from Him. They are like the ark of the covenant in the tabernacle that was moved over to the temple that was built by Solomon. Sure, the tent was done away with. It shifted in shape and form. However, the furnishings made of gold remained.

These first precepts that God gives you will always remain the core of your mandate. The very things that you base your ministry and future on. Do you remember the day you got such a conviction? For me, it was the day the Lord said that Craig and I would be spiritual parents. It was the day He told me that our lives were not our own and that we would never settle in one place.

It was when He said that all we were and would go through was to accumulate the anointing and strengths that others would need. Whether we train fivefold ministers, minister inner healing, or mentor other apostles, the core remains the same.

We are parents. We are mentors. We are trainers. We are missionaries. We are a living sacrifice, meant to be filled up and poured out so that we can make the Church a city on a hill. Our instruction is to walk in meticulous obedience, to trust God with all our strength and to "lean not on our own understanding."

What are your Ten Commandments?

What foundational precepts has God given you through the years? If you look through your journey, you will see those commandments again and again. The same message. The same scriptures. These are your commandments, and the rest of the pattern that you are about to receive will hang off of these.

> *Everything else might change, but these commandments will always remain. They are the core of your apostolic mandate.*

Establishing Organization: The Law and Ordinances

You see, there are more details. There are more pieces of the puzzle. If you go through Leviticus and Exodus, you will see exactly how many different concepts and different laws the Lord gave Moses. They were categorized one by one and laid out very systematically.

The Lord showed him and said, "This is how you deal with a murderer. This is how you give me sacrifices. This is how you deal with the false prophet. This is how you deal with cleanliness."

Every little ordinance was laid out, one principle at a time, expanded and explained and put in its place. Moses spent all that time getting this information bit by bit, and slowly, the picture started becoming clear.

Angel Assigned to Your Ministry

Now the Lord gave Moses another promise here. He said to him, "An angel will go before you, and he is going to prepare the way. He will lay everything out."

> ***Exodus 23:20*** *"Behold, I send an Angel before you to keep you in the way and to bring you into the place which I have prepared.*
>
> *21 Beware of Him and obey His voice; do not provoke Him, for He will not pardon your transgressions; for My name is in Him.*

The Lord has an angel assigned to you. There is an angel assigned to every apostle – at least one – to go ahead and prepare the way and to make sure things fall into place to bring everything to pass. The Lord has had this plan set up before the beginning of time. You just need to walk the path that has been laid for you a long time ago.

You see, this path has been prepared for you. Now the Lord has been waiting for you to catch up and to get to the place where He can now put you on this path, so that you can start walking.

That is what all the preparation and death has been about - to make you ready to be placed on this path. The angel of the Lord has already gone ahead of you and prepared the way, and all those pieces of the puzzle are right there along this road. All you need to do is put your head down and keep on walking. They will come to pass in the Lord's time.

God is in Control

God is truly in control of your calling, your ministry, and your life. You are not in control of your destiny, nor your ministry. At this stage, God is in control!

> *Your responsibility is to keep walking and to keep climbing.*

If you have submitted your life to the Lord and to the cross and finally come to this part, don't fret about how you are going to do it. Don't fret about what is going to become of your ministry, who is to be in it, or what you are going to do about it. God is in control.

This is His ministry! This is His calling. These are His people, and He will lead them His way! He just happens to be using you to do it. You just happen to be the vessel. The path, the plan, and the pattern are all His. They are all set in place and ready to go. You are just the instrument that will reveal this plan to His people.

So, do not think, "What if I miss it? What if I get it wrong? What if I didn't plan it properly?"

The plan has already been set in motion. You just make sure that you are the best vessel that you can be. Make sure that your heart is where it should be, and that you are in order.

God will take care of the people, the plan, the action, the "how-tos" and the "what ifs." You just take care of yourself and make sure that you are walking on that straight and narrow road. Make sure that you are putting one foot in front of the other and that you are heading up that mountain. That is all you need to worry about. He will deal with you when you get there. Just make sure you get there.

That is all that God is calling you to do right now. He is not calling you to understand it, figure it out, or to help Him along with His plan. He can handle it. He has it together. He is the best architect there is. He doesn't need your help. All He needs is you, His vessel, so that He can take the plan that is already there and reveal it to His people through you.

So, in the fourth visit, the plans are laid out. Suddenly, everything starts making sense, and Moses now has a solid foundation for the people of Israel.

Even if he had to be taken right now, they would have something to go on. They have the Law and the Ten Commandments. They have all the ordinances. They know what to do, when to do it, and how to do it. It is all nicely laid out in a structure. The full picture is starting to come into place now. They have the principles now but lack something vital to make them come alive.

They lack the power.

THE 5TH VISIT: IMPARTATION

Now there comes the fifth visit. Let's look at Exodus 24:9-10. It says:

> *Then Moses went up, also Aaron, Nadab, and Abihu, and seventy of the elders of Israel,*
>
> *10 and they saw the God of Israel. And there was under His feet as it were a paved work of sapphire stone, and it was like the very heavens in its clarity.*

It is time to get practical! You have the vision, fire, and instruction from God, but you will realize sooner than later that you cannot do the job alone.

And so, the fifth climb is a time when you take the leaders with you. This really amazed me, because growing up and just reading my illustrated bible story book, I imagined Moses being the only one who saw God. That is not true! Aaron, two of his sons, and the seventy elders saw God too.

Moses took them up with him the fifth time he climbed the mountain and introduced them to the Father. They didn't just see the fire and the lightning like the rest of the congregation. They saw God!

You say, "What? You mean the apostle isn't the only one to have the secret relationship with God? He is not on a higher spiritual plane than everybody else that nobody can attain to?"

You are meant to be preparing the way ahead, apostle. If the leaders that follow cannot attain to what you have, then you are not doing your job properly. It is not just the apostle that is meant to have a relationship with the Father. We just pave the way. We just get things ready and go ahead to tell people how to get there. We climb the mountain and then show them how to do it for themselves.

The first people Moses took were Aaron, his sons, and the seventy elders. And so, in the same way, you will take those that are under your care and those whom the Lord desires to raise up as leaders. You will take them with you into the presence of the Father, and you will introduce them to Him.

PARTAKING OF THE POWER

They will not only see the Father, but they will start partaking of the anointing that is on your life. They will start functioning and acting in that anointing. They will start having experiences with the Father for themselves.

That is the way it is meant to be. It must pour down from you. Sure, you hold a position of authority. Yet, they should be functioning with the same anointing that you are functioning in.

Don't hog it all to yourself and say, "Well, this is my experience with the Father, and that is the way it is going to be."

Then, you go out and tell everybody about these magnificent experiences you have had and how spiritually exalted you are because you had these experiences with the Father. You share how anointed you are.

It becomes a case of, "*My* anointing, *my* gifts, and *my* calling."

No, they are God's gifts! It is God's anointing and calling, and you have been called to share it with the rest of the body of Christ.

The position of authority might be yours, however, the anointing belongs to God's people. Don't dare hog it to yourself! That is the mistake that many have made in the body of Christ up until this time.

For centuries now, God has been revealing the truth. He has revealed Himself to man. But, instead of spreading that anointing, man keeps it to himself and exalts himself above everyone - sitting on a higher spiritual plane.

Jesus did not do that. Jesus was given the fullness of the anointing of the Father, and while He walked this earth, He gave that anointing to His disciples.

He said, "You have seen me raise the dead and heal the sick. Now freely give what you have freely received. (Matt 10:8)"

While He was still walking the earth, He sent His disciples off to do the exact same thing that He was doing.

He had the authority. He led them and protected them and was their covering sure enough, but they did the exact same miracles that Jesus did. When it came to the power, they were on the same level.

Isn't that the way it should be? I cannot have one kind of blood flowing through my hand and have a different kind of blood flowing through my foot. It is the same blood that flows through my whole body.

ANOINTING OSMOSIS

How can you have one kind of anointing in your hand and another kind in your foot and there not be a transfusion or osmosis taking place that makes you share the same anointing?

It should be something natural. If you are in a ministry and are pouring into the leaders that God has given you, they should be functioning in your anointing. They should be speaking like you speak. They should be hearing like you hear. They should be ministering like you minister.

If they are not, then you have failed as a leader because you have not taken them to the Father. You have not introduced them to the Father. You have kept it all to yourself. It is not God's order.

> *It is God's order that you go up to receive the anointing and then share it.*

Jesus Gave Everything

Is that not what Jesus did? As He died upon the cross, He went and took the keys of death and hell. Then, He ascended to the Father. He climbed the mountain one last time! He ascended to the Father, and then what did He do?

He brought the Father to the people and said, "As the Father sent me, so send I you. As the Father anointed me, I went and received the fullness. In my name, you will cast out demons. In my name, you have power over all the principalities of darkness. You do it in my name! My name has been given that power and authority, and now I am giving it to you. You can have the fullness. Here it is – the whole lot!"

Jesus held nothing back! He breathed the Holy Spirit into them, and they received the fullness of everything that He had received from the Father! He even gave them His authority to use.

Distribution of Power

That is what God is calling us to do. We are to take what we receive on the mountain and pour it out to the Church. We are to bring the Father to the people. We are to introduce them to Him, so that they can see Him for themselves.

We live in a church era where everybody is taught to feed off the apostle, the prophet, the pastor, or teacher. They never grow up to go and feed themselves. They never learn to rise up and touch God for themselves.

This is the biggest mistake that the children of Israel made. They kept on saying, "Moses, we'll talk to God through you."

They said to him, "We're too afraid to come into the presence of the Father. So, I tell you what, Moses, you speak to the Father, and then you speak to us. You can be the mediator."

MAKING THE INTRODUCTION

This is the first step, and it is good. When a baby comes into the body of Christ, they don't know how to approach the Father, and you are that point of contact for them. You are the facilitator, so to speak, and you introduce them.

You start showing them the way. You start giving them principles until they can get on their baby feet and start walking. The whole idea is to teach them how to access the Father for themselves, not to keep them from Him. The idea is for you to go up and bring it down to the people, and for them to experience His power for themselves.

This is the apostolic era in which we live. This is what the apostles of God are called to do for the body of Christ. Their ultimate calling is to bring God to His people. They are to introduce the Bride to the Groom so that a marriage can take place. No longer is the Bride going to go through the best man to speak to the Groom. We are called to make an introduction.

LET'S ARRANGE A MARRIAGE

You know, in ages past, a father would take his daughter, and he would arrange her marriage. The parents would introduce the couple, and then they would be married. Sometimes, they would only meet for the first time on their wedding day.

That is what we are kind of called to do as apostles. We are to take the bride of Christ, and we are to take the Lord and introduce the two. First, we must know who the Father is.

You can't tell a bride, "You know he's so good-looking. He's got blue eyes," if you don't even know what the guy looks like.

You can't convince this bride that this is somebody she wants to marry if you don't know the man yourself.

So, you have a lovely example of Rebekah and how Jacob had sent his servant out and said, "Go, and find my son a wife."

So, he went to her family, and now he had to explain what kind of man Isaac was and what kind of family he came from. He had to make it sound really good so that she would go back with him. He really painted a good picture.

He said, "He's rich. He's wonderful. He's good-looking," and he laid it on real thick.

She said, "Hey, this sounds like a pretty good deal. Take me."

So, he took Rebekah and introduced her to Isaac, and they were married.

That is a picture of what you are doing, but first, you need to get into a relationship with the Father and know who He is. Once you know who He is, and once you know His glory, then you can introduce that glory to the body of Christ and make them want it.

You must make them want to look upon it and not fear it.

So, on the fifth visit, you will take up the leaders with you. Before the people experience it, the leaders must experience it, otherwise, it will not filter down from there. You see, it is like a pyramid. It starts with you, then it goes to the leaders, and then to the rest of the body of Christ.

BEGIN WITH THE LEADERS

You know what we have happening in many ministries these days? You have one leader who is experiencing everything, and he is keeping it all to himself.

He will maybe share it with the general congregation, but those leaders who are under him are as dry as can be. They don't experience anything! No, first you must introduce those leaders to the Father, and then they, in turn, will introduce Him to the people.

A solid foundation will be built – one that cannot be shaken and that will remain.

CHAPTER 12

6TH VISIT:
THE TABERNACLE

Chapter 12 – 6ᵀᴴ Visit: The Tabernacle

> **Exodus 25:8** *And let them make Me a sanctuary, that I may dwell among them.*
>
> *9 According to all that I show you, that is, the pattern of the tabernacle and the pattern of all its furnishings, just so you shall make it.*

Set in Stone

Forty days and forty nights. That is how long Moses remained up the mountain this time. Piece by piece, the Lord started to give him one of the most revolutionary patterns for the children of Israel.

A pattern that would be a type and shadow of the New Testament to come. A pattern that would continue for generations, bring about wars, times of peace, and literally, shape the history of nations.

During Moses' sixth ascent, the Lord gave Moses the pattern for the Tabernacle and carved the Law in stone with His hand.

All the patterns that the Lord had been giving Moses up until now, He carved in stone with His hand, and then He gave Moses the pattern for the tabernacle.

The foundation had been laid. Now comes the grand finale - the full picture and the setting in place of what is to come.

I will just say that at this stage, the sixth visit, Moses had started entering into a much more personal relationship with the Father. He knew who He was. He felt who He was, and he was becoming confident and bold.

He was changing and transforming continually now from image to image. Soon, you are not going to be able to tell the difference between Moses and the Father because they are becoming one.

Transformation

You see a total change in Moses' character, from the burning bush to where you see him getting really angry with the children of Israel! So, there was a change coming with each time he went up. He was leaving more behind and bringing more down.

That is what is happening with you. You are being called to deeper death, deeper sacrifice, and deeper commitment. With each sacrifice and each commitment, you come down the mountain with something greater and more magnificent.

So, you are going from stage to stage, from glory to glory, until that cloud starts to form around you. Soon, you will not be able to tell the vessel from the glory. You won't be able to tell the father from the child.

The Full Picture

This is what you are heading towards. You will receive the pattern for the structure that is to be upon your foundation - the crowning glory. You will begin to put all the pieces together. Suddenly, everything will make sense!

You will now start going from theory into practice and will apply everything you have received. Up until this time, it has been a case of getting the picture and getting the teaching, the understanding, and the knowledge.

You have been thinking, "Am I here or there? Am I up or down? Where on earth am I? Am I supposed to be leading them to the land of milk and honey, or am I supposed to be spending all my time writing out all this Law?

"Am I supposed to be building the tent? Am I supposed to be laying an altar and offering sacrifices, or am I supposed to be giving them festivals? What am I supposed to be doing?"

SO MANY DIRECTIONS

It seems that just when you are just comfortable with one thing, the Lord has you on another track. And so, you will get a job and get to understand a certain concept and principle. Then, you will suddenly be off into another job or ministry, and it feels like you are playing hopscotch.

You think, "Wow, this is a powerful revelation! So, this is what the Lord has for the prophets. This is wonderful! I can't wait to apply it."

The Lord says, "No, I'm leading you to do more teaching now."

You say, "Okay, that's great."

The Lord did this with us. We thought, "Wow, so this is what the teaching ministry is about! Let's go get it, and do it. Let's get the teachers together!"

The Lord said, "No, I just wanted you to understand it. Now, I want you to understand the pastor."

Just when we got a little zealous, when the penny finally dropped about the pastoral ministry, and we wanted to get going, He said, "No, not yet. There are still a couple more I want you to do."

You seem to be jumping everywhere, and sure, by the end of it, you will have understood a lot. You will have seen a lot. You have gotten a lot of pattern and a lot of principles. You have a magnificent blueprint, but there is still no building.

You say, "I'd like to start putting up this building now."

You've got a blueprint, and it's great. The Lord has put all the pieces in place. You have a full-scale model right there, but now starts coming the time when the Lord says, "Okay, now it is time to put this thing into practice. This isn't just a scaled down model anymore. Now, you are going to do the real thing!"

FITTING EVERYTHING TOGETHER

On the sixth visit, the whole picture is put together. Within the pattern for the Tabernacle, we see everything coming together - all the ordinances and the Ten Commandments.

Suddenly, you can see where everything fits in, and why the Lord gave the Laws and ordinances that He did. Just look at the Tabernacle and how it was constructed, how everything was put together, and what was used in it. It falls so perfectly in line with all the laws that the Lord had been giving Moses time after time.

Suddenly all the pieces of the puzzle start fitting together, and you start getting the full picture. You finally grasp it with your hands, and everything moves from theory to practical application.

It is time to set Aaron and his sons in place and to build. Can you see the process that you have been through so far? It was not a call you received "because someone prophesied it over you!"

No, this is a living, breathing mandate that God has been expanding over the years. Each time when you thought it was time for the full picture, you were called up the mountain again to get another piece.

However, with each climb, the vessel you are changed. The anointing increased. Your wisdom increased. Finally, you are becoming the vessel God requires to build His Tabernacle.

Are you coming to the realization yet that this call depends on God and not on you? So many tout the "Apostle" title, not realizing the kind of legwork required to fulfill it.

It is so much more than having authority. It is so much more than having good doctrine. It is even more than having an encounter with God. It means having a God-given mandate that houses that authority, power, and revelation so that God's house can be built in the world!

The Lord has called you to build something that remains and that houses all of the fivefold ministry, body ministries, advancement of the kingdom of God, edification of the saints, and [YOUR VISION HERE].

This process has been equipping you and giving you the pattern to house and establish God's will in the earth. It is no surprise that to rise up into the apostolic call takes years. It is not just about experience and power. It is about taking the time to receive the pattern to build… God's way.

THE REBELLION

Anyone who takes the time to step away from the ministry and leave it in the care of others understands full well the risk you take and the tests your leaders will face. This is exactly what happened as Moses spent the longest time ever on that mountain.

The children of Israel built a golden calf! It feels as if the enemy throws one last hurdle at you to discourage you from building. How Moses must have felt! One understands his dramatic burst of emotion as he hurls the tablets of stone down the mountain.

How many times have you put your ministry in the care of others, only for them to fail you? I am here to say that not all is lost though. Neither is this the end of the journey. I will teach you a bit more of this in the next chapter, but for now, there is something else you need to know.

There is one more climb you need to make, one more visit that you need to build the pattern you have. You need more than mandates and patterns and ordinances. You need the manifest power of God.

THE 7TH VISIT: THE MANIFEST POWER OF GOD

> *Exodus 33:18 And he said, "Please, show me Your glory."*
>
> *19 Then He said, "I will make all My goodness pass before you, and I will proclaim the name of the Lord before you. I*

will be gracious to whom I will be gracious, and I will have compassion on whom I will have compassion."

20 But He said, "You cannot see My face; for no man shall see Me, and live."

21 And the Lord said, "Here is a place by Me, and you shall stand on the rock.

22 So it shall be, while My glory passes by, that I will put you in the cleft of the rock, and will cover you with My hand while I pass by.

23 Then I will take away My hand, and you shall see My back; but My face shall not be seen."

Exodus 34:29 *Now it was so, when Moses came down from Mount Sinai (and the two tablets of the Testimony were in Moses' hand when he came down from the mountain), that Moses did not know that the skin of his face shone while he talked with Him.*

Moses is called to the mountain one last time - the seventh time. Once again, he remained for forty days and nights. As you have joined me at the "burning bush" experience and followed me through each ascent, you have begun to see how much more time Moses spent with the Father.

You get the idea that the more anointing and authority an apostle has, the less they need to be alone with the Lord. However, the opposite is true. The more you grow, the more time you need to be separated to be changed, filled, and transformed.

This time, when Moses returned from the mountain, his face was shining with the glory!

He came down a completed vessel. He came down not just as a pot or a pan or any other kind of vessel. He came down after the glory had enveloped the vessel that he was, and what you saw was not the vessel - but the glory.

Moses truly saw God, the Father, face-to-face. He had an experience upon that mountaintop that transformed him physically.

Up until now, the Lord has been working on you internally. He has been working on your inner needs, your templates, your inner sacrifices and motivations, and He has been weeding out all those things. He will do a lot of it through the Word. He has been changing the templates. Even with Moses, we see how He was doing that. He was displacing everything.

You see, Moses had grown up in Egypt. He had all these ideas of how a nation should be led, how things should be built, and how they should be done. Having been exposed to all the Egyptian gods and how they worshipped, he would have had many preconceived ideas.

So, the Lord brought every preconceived idea down. Every time he went up and got a new ordinance from the Ten Commandments to receiving the pattern for the Tabernacle, God replaced wrong ideas with right ones.

Your Apostolic Transformation

There is so much more for you to look forward to as you ascend just one more time (for this mandate anyway!)

You will go up with all your sacred cows. You will go up with what you think you should do, how God's people should be led, and how you should put this ministry together.

Each time you go up, God will say, "Okay, let's replace this one. We'll smash that one. Leave it behind at the bottom of the mountain. I'm replacing it with a new template."

So, you will go through a complete inner renovation. This is going to be a real deeply changing time for you, where you are going to realize, "I had a sinful template. I had that preconceived idea, and that wrong mindset."

I remember the Lord taking me through this time, and I was so shocked. I thought, "Okay, enough of the template dealing already. I've had enough of this!"

He said, "I am going to show you that there are templates in your life related to ministry. They are old templates and misconceptions that need to die."

I had grown up as a pastor's kid. I had grown up in church. I was ministering in the worship band at the age of thirteen. I didn't realize I had bad templates, but I did. I had built up templates for ministry of how I thought things should be run, of how things were done out there.

They had formed my thinking, but God said, "I don't want them to be done like that. I want it to change. I want it to be different."

So came a time of chopping, and changing, and replacing, where He exposed all my wrong attitudes.

He said, "You see pastors through your own preconceived ideas, but this is not really what a pastor is. This isn't what the pastoral ministry is about. You have a wrong mindset."

He would smash it and replace it with the correct one.

He said, "This is what you think worship is. Wrong!"

He would smash it and replace it with something else.

He said, "This is what you think a church structure should look like. It's wrong!", and He smashed it and replaced it with something else.

A Visible Change

One at a time, each incorrect mindset will be broken and replaced, until the time comes when you enter into the presence of the Father. It will no longer just be a "heart thing." In fact, it will not even be a spirit or a soul change anymore, but it will start reflecting through your body.

It will reflect in the way you speak, the way you stand, and the way you minister. It will even reflect through the way you act, or through the way you write. In everything you do, you will not be able to help yourself, because the glory of God will shine on your face so much that people will notice it. You will be visibly changed.

You will not need to convince people and say, "You know God has changed me so much."

You will say, "Hi," and they'll say, "What happened to you?"

It will show on you visibly. You will not be the same person.

Have you ever heard people who say, "Well, this is just the way I am. Accept me as I am."?

It is not good enough! You will not "be just as you are." You will become a vessel for His glory, and you will change physically. From your body language and your speech to the way you hold yourself – it will all change!

The way you minister will change. The way you speak to people and confront them or love them will change. It must change! You must represent the King of Kings. You must represent the Father.

> *When you stand up, you must look like the Father. You must reflect the glory of the Father. You must not reflect your own insecurities, your own needs, or your inability.*

You must stand and reflect the glory of the Father. When you reflect the glory of the Father, you would have taken the Father from the mountain, and you would have brought Him down to the people. Now, you are ready to introduce the Father to the people.

So, Moses came down, and he put together the Tabernacle and laid out all the Laws. He wrote them all down. This time, he had to do all the hard work. All the Lord did the second time around was the Ten Commandments with His hand. Poor Moses had to do the rest himself this time.

He wrote it all down and set it all up, and what do we have here? We have the glory cloud in the tent! Moses took what he experienced on the mountain, what he saw and lived on the mountain, and he put it together in the Tabernacle.

That was the Holy of Holies. He brought the mountain down to the people. That is why you have to climb the mountain, so that you can bring the mountain to the people. Can you see the power in this whole process?

MY PERSONAL ENCOUNTER

The Lord gave me a vision once, and I didn't understand it until I came to put this teaching together. He showed me how I had come into the secret place, where I always had intimate experiences with Him in the Spirit. There were things that He showed me that I did not share with anybody!

So, there I was having this experience with Him. It was as if I had come out of darkness and into this place of light, and it was just Him and me. We would commune face-to-face, and He would share things with me, and just pour into me. We would bounce things off each other. It was a face-to-face, personal, daily encounter.

Then He said to me one day as I arrived in our secret place, "It is time to leave."

I said, "No! This is where I belong. This is where I'm comfortable."

He said, "It's not good enough. You have to take this to the people now."

It was as if I was in a room with Him, and all around was darkness. I used to hide myself in this glory, in this golden room. All I remember is everything being gold.

I was in there. We were talking, and He said, "You must go out."

As I stepped out of the lit room, it was dark outside. I looked up and saw that I was holding His hand. The Lord was shining brightly in the darkness. As I looked at my hands and arms, I saw that I was also shining with the same glory that was in that room.

As we were holding hands, I saw a blood transfusion from His vein to mine, through our wrists. It was like that same blood was pumping through both of us – symbolic of Him pouring His life into me.

It was a symbol of me being Him, and Him being in me, and through me. As we walked in this darkness which was the world, the light remained, and we brought everything with us that I had been experiencing in my private time.

He said to me, "You can't keep this to yourself. You must take it to the people."

This is what the Moses apostle does. He takes the experiences that he has, and he brings it down to the people, so that, at any time, they can go into the tabernacle and inquire of the Lord for themselves.

Once everything had been set up, the people could go in at any time and experience God for themselves.

We see Joshua doing just that. He used to spend hour upon hour in the presence of the Father, long after Moses left the presence of God. He could do that because Moses had brought the glory down.

The people could go and inquire of God and say, "Should I do this? Should I do that?" because the cloud was there. His presence was there. They could touch Him. Suddenly, they were no longer fearful and had to go through Moses to touch God all of the time. They could come to the Father for themselves.

That was the Old Covenant in a limited way, but in the New Covenant, in the blood covenant of Christ, people could enter into a face-to-face relationship with the Lord greater than even Moses had!

THE INCREASE IN CHRIST

Moses could not see or touch God because he was a sinful creature. Yet, through Christ, and through the washing of His Blood, we can come into a relationship with the Father face-to-face and experience Him at a much more intimate level than what Moses ever had.

We can hear Him speaking to us every day. We don't have to wait. We can close our eyes and experience Him any time we want to. It comes from climbing the mountain a couple of times.

If you, as an apostle, can climb the mountain and take the time to enter into that relationship, that relationship will remain with you for all time. Then, you would have cut the path ahead and blazed a trail for others to come and experience that relationship as well.

Then, it will not be a once-off experience. It won't be one little revival meeting where you say, "Oh, the glory was there! The cloud was there and now it is time to go home…"

No. The glory of God will be with us twenty-four hours a day! It will be a fire at night and a cloud during the day. His cloud will be surrounding the body of Christ all the time. They can touch God any time they please.

It is going to shatter this world and shake the foundations of this earth! It comes with your sacrifice though. You have to climb the mountain. You have to bring it to God's people. You have to experience it, know it, and feel it for yourself before you can give it to them.

Can you sense the awesome responsibility that God has placed in your hands? This isn't about giving a couple of sermons. This isn't about starting a ministry. This certainly is not about having a title in front of your name.

This is about bringing the Father to His people, and the people to their Father. This is about experiencing the manifest glory of God that is our promise in these end-times. It is about bringing that glory to the people.

I want you to reach out now as I pray.

A Call to Climb – A Prophetic Decree

I see the mountain in the Spirit, and it is shaking and quaking. The cloud has come down, and the Father is saying, *"It is you! I am calling you, now stand up and climb the mountain."*

Upon that mountain, you will experience the Father face-to-face. You will see Him face-to-face. I call forth a revelation right now of the Father. I speak it upon you.

> *Father, I pray that you would manifest yourself to your people. Right now, speak to them. Let them hear you. Let them feel you. Let them feel that shaking, that quivering, right within the center of them.*
>
> *Let them know that the Father speaks, for the Father is calling His apostles. The Father is calling His vessels, that they would rise up and that they would minister to His Body. He is calling them to rise up and take His authority, and His power, and bring His glory down to His people.*
>
> *For the Father is saying to every apostle, "Stand up and be counted, for the time has come when I will raise up my Bride as a magnificent and fearsome vessel in the sight of the nations.*
>
> *It is you, apostle, that shall make my Bride such a magnificent vessel! It is you that shall make her so awesome. It is you that shall make her so fearsome. It is you that will bring my fear and my awe and my power, for the time of the lamb is over, and the time of the lion has come!*
>
> *We shall indeed take the kingdom of God by force, and it shall be in power, and it shall be in authority! It shall be in*

thunder and lightning, and brimstone, for there shall be no more gentle words, but the words shall be strong.

It shall no longer be a gentle move. It shall no longer move slowly and build up to a momentum, for the momentum is here, says the Lord. You live in the momentum, and you are breathing in the momentum, and you will call that momentum forth in my Church.

They shall rise up as warriors in power and in awe, and there shall be no doubt in the sight of the world that this is my warrior whom I have called to rise up. This is my Bride. This is my chosen vessel, and they will fear her just as the Egyptians feared Moses and the Israelites. They shall rally to her for they will fear her.

They shall no longer look upon her with scorn, but they shall fear her. For they will know that the hand of the Almighty God, the God of all gods, rests upon this vessel. They will know that Almighty God's Spirit is upon this vessel, and they are to be feared. For I am an awesome and fearful God.

You shall raise her up in this awe, says the Lord. This is what I am calling you to do. Now rise up and come to the mountain and take this of my hand."

Chapter 13

Handling a Rebellious Generation

Chapter 13 – Handling a Rebellious Generation

As I have been looking at the move of the Spirit in recent times, one thing has become very clear. Before we can enter into the fullness of what the Lord has for us, change needs to come about first.

Thing is – it's so much easier to see how everyone else needs to change. Sit in any church, at any given time, and every person will have an opinion on how the pastor can do it better.

Are you any different? As an apostle, you already have a desire to change the Church, so you look around at what needs to be repaired. You see leaders and pastors that need to change, so that the Holy Spirit can be given license in the earth.

Plenty of good ideas and revelation for everyone else's ministry. However, what are you doing right now that makes you any different?

Change Starts With You

Yes… everyone has wisdom when it comes to everybody else's ministry. However, do you know what? The buck stops here! It stops right here with me, and with you.

If you want to change the world, you need to start with… you! If you want to break down the walls in others, you start with yourself. Until you can see clearly, and until you can get revelation without preconceived ideas, your words will be useless and empty.

Until you look in the mirror, nobody will listen to you because your words do not carry authority, and they do not carry experience. Above all, they do not carry the anointing of the Holy Spirit.

> *Before you can preach it, you must have lived it.*
> *Before you can teach it, you must have received it yourself.*

That is where we are today. We are not playing fun and games. This is the kingdom of God we are talking about! We are not here to give pretty prophecies, dance around, and "bring down the Spirit."

We are here to bring change, but people don't like change. If you are to get them to change, it starts with you. If you are not willing to change, what makes you think you will get them to change? All you are wanting to do is to make them think like you do.

Perhaps you are thinking, "I have the revelation here. I'm the prophet, I'm the apostle. The Lord's given me the mandate. They must think like me."

However, until you are willing to change your ideals, your mindsets, and your preconceived ideas, you have no room to talk. So, before we stand and shout our mouths off at everybody else, let's take a good hard look at ourselves.

When I compare the Moses and the Davidic apostolic types I think, "Lord, may I be Davidic?"

Moses had it tough! David was the conquering hero, and the mighty warriors gave their lives for him. But, the people wanted to stone poor Moses every five minutes. I think he had the toughest job of them all.

In my flesh, I wouldn't want to lead that bunch of people if you paid me! Yet, when God puts that mantle on you, it becomes your mandate and your call. Regardless of the price, we pick it up and carry it because it is a fire within us that cannot be quenched!

PEOPLE ARE STILL STIFF-NECKED

Now, there are some in these times whom the Lord is raising up to be Moses apostles. If you are one of them, you will be handling a rebellious generation. They will be people who are stiff-necked and do not want to change. They will be people who are used to the old way of doing things.

In this chapter, I would like to discuss some points on how to break those stiff necks, perhaps shatter some templates and bring about a bit of change. However, before you take what I have to say and apply it to the hearts of others, I want you to apply it to yourself first because the change starts with you. Acts 7:51-53 says:

> *"You stiff-necked and uncircumcised in heart and ears! You always resist the Holy Spirit; as your fathers did, so do you.*
>
> *52 Which of the prophets did your fathers not persecute? And they killed those who foretold the coming of the Just One, of whom you now have become the betrayers and murderers,*
>
> *53 who have received the law by the direction of angels and have not kept it."*

This word was given to the Pharisees, and it is the same word that was given to the Israelites in the wilderness. You would think that after a few hundred years, they would have changed a little. You would think that two thousand years later, in today's modern age, people would have changed a little…

Reality check! People have not changed that much at all! We are still stiff-necked. We are still rebellious. We still hanker after the leeks of Egypt and continue to look back while trying to walk forward.

If you are called to be a Moses apostle, realize that you have your task cut out for you because you will be confrontational, you will be strong, and you will get in people's faces.

You will also be doing a whole lot of smashing. That is your main responsibility as a Moses apostle. It is to smash the mindsets and templates, and to replace them with the new, so that you might prepare the people for the Promised Land, and for the move of God that is to come.

How will you prepare them? How are you going to convince a bunch of stiff-necked people that they have to change? Have you ever gotten into an argument with somebody to try and convince them that what you know is right? Did you try to tell them that your revelation is the way to go?

Have you ever tried to get somebody who just doesn't understand - to get it? It is impossible! In our own human understanding, and in our own human ability, it is impossible. You see, that is why we have the Holy Spirit, and He is what makes everything different.

Hearts Must Be Ready to Receive

The first thing you need to realize is that the Lord will send you when the people's hearts are ready. Don't think that it is because of your great ability and anointing that the Lord raised you up out of the ashes. Don't think that it is because you are so wonderful that you were called up out of obscurity.

It was the cry of God's people that raised up Moses. It is the cry of God's people today that are raising up the prophets and apostles. It has nothing to do with you.

It is not because of your faith or your anointing. It is because of their prayers of faith, crying out to God night after night saying, "Father, my heart needs change. Father, this church has to change. I can't go on like this anymore. Send us a deliverer."

Their hearts have to be ready first. That is what happens when you are in the backside of the desert. Moses thought he would take things into his own hands at the beginning. We all know how that ended up. He ended up killing an Egyptian and running for his life.

Newsflash: You're Going Back

Why? The people's hearts were not yet ready. You have seen this. You have seen what has happened as you have stood up to deliver a word. You know it. You have been criticized, kicked out of churches, and ridiculed. Their hearts were not ready to receive.

Moses thought he would stand up and say, "Your deliverer has come. Hello Israel, here I come."

They looked at him and said, "Who do you think you are? You little upstart, little rich kid, sitting in the palace, now you want to come and tell us what to do? You have no idea what it is like to be a slave! You have no idea what it even means to put in a day's work, and you want to come and talk to me?"

So, the Lord put him in the backside of the desert for a little while to calm him down. He taught Moses a few principles about work and getting his hands dirty, and what it meant to look after some smelly sheep.

He started learning a few lessons. As he was learning a few of these lessons, the hearts of God's people were being prepared. Their hearts were becoming hungry. They were crying out to the Lord and saying, "Lord, you have to send us a deliverer!"

Only then did the Lord send Moses back to the children of Israel.

As you have been sitting in the backside of the desert, you have been wondering, "Lord, did I miss it? I just don't even want to think about them! They gave me such a hard time. I don't want to go back. What do I want to go back to that horrible church for? They kicked me out and called me a Jezebel. Why must I go back and speak to them again?"

You see, as much as He has been preparing your heart, He has been preparing theirs. When their hearts are ready to receive, He will send you back.

This is something we overlook so much. We think that our words will bring readiness to their hearts, but this is not so.

Who changes the heart? The Holy Spirit does it. If you are sitting in the backside of the desert, that is what you should be praying.

You should be praying, "Lord, change the hearts of your people," because when their hearts are ready, He will send you to speak the word. Then, when you speak, they will listen.

When Moses was sent – he arrived with signs and wonders. The people recognized him and followed him. There was no doubt that now was the time.

1ˢᵀ Step: Exposing the System

The first step that Moses took in leading the children of Israel out of Egypt is that he exposed the system. Even in today's society, the Church is in a system, and I can guarantee that you are aware of that system.

You can see it. You can see the flaws in it. You can see what is wrong with it, and you look at everybody sitting in those pews and say, "Why don't they get it?"

So many times people have said to me, "Why don't they get it? Can't they see it?"

No, they can't see! You are expecting them to see something that they cannot see. They cannot see, and they cannot hear. They have not received the revelation. It is not in their hearts. You have the revelation, but they don't. They are not being rebellious. They really just don't get it.

So, the first thing Moses had to do was expose the system, and so… came the plagues. The Israelites saw the Egyptians as a mighty nation. They trembled because the Egyptians were such a mighty nation. Pharaoh was like a god, so Moses had to bring Pharaoh down a few notches first.

He had to humiliate him in the sight of the Israelites so that they could look and say, "Actually the system isn't so great. Egypt is not as strong as we thought."

You see, all they had seen were the slave-drivers and Pharaoh who looked so big and ominous. The system looked so tremendous. As the plagues of Egypt began, they started seeing things for the first time in their lives.

Jesus did the same thing when He began His ministry. You read in the New Testament of how He didn't mince His words when it came to the Pharisees.

> **Matthew 23:27** *Woe to you, scribes and Pharisees, hypocrites! For you are like whitewashed tombs which indeed appear beautiful outwardly, but inside are full of dead men's bones and all uncleanness.*

I have always wondered why the Lord was so harsh with the Pharisees. I have always believed that the Lord gives us correction so that we will change our ways. Yet, as I read the Word, the Pharisees never changed their ways.

So, did He just get into a fighting match with them for the fun of it because He could not help Himself? Why did He berate the Pharisees continually? Because their hearts never changed. They did not repent, and they didn't accept Him as the Messiah, so why did He even bother?

Exposure Through Humiliation

I tell you why He bothered. It was because He had to humiliate those Pharisees in the sight of all the people, so that they would let go of the tradition and the bondage that the Pharisees had put them under. The Pharisees had made so many laws, and the people had to carry heavy burdens.

The Lord said as much to them. He said, "You put heavy burdens on God's people that you yourself are not willing to bear." (Matt 23:4)

You see, in the eyes of the people, the Pharisees were a representation of God. They were the bringers of the law. They were the law! Before the Lord Jesus could come and bring change and a new gospel, He had to kill the old, and He had to expose it for what it was. He made a fool of those Pharisees. He made a laughing stock of them.

The people stood up and thought, "Hang on a minute. They're not so wonderful. Actually, they are just as rotten as we are."

Whereas before they thought the Pharisees were so holy, and so one with God, now they started thinking, "Actually, they're stinking, rotten sinners! Look at them. They're whitewashed tombs!" The people lost respect for them.

Now, the minute that system started being exposed, and the minute the people started losing respect for the hierarchy, Jesus could step in with the gospel of grace and change the hearts of the people. They saw the flaws, they saw the fallacy, and what happened? They were set free from the bondage of their hearts and minds. They could see clearly.

Now, this is what the Moses apostle will have to do in the system. He will have to come face-to-face with the Pharisees. You see, nobody likes to rock the boat, and that is why the Moses apostle is usually older in years, more mature and confident.

He has to be because he has to rock the boat. He has to take that rod and smash the foundation that has been incorrectly laid. He is called to tear down.

That is quite a call. You must have quite a strong character to be able to do that because you are going to be coming face-to-face with pastors, with leaders, and with Pharisees who are not walking according to the Word and will of God. They are leading the people astray and putting them under bondage to religion and heresy.

You are going to have to confront them and deal with it. So, if you feel that the Lord has put a Moses calling on your heart, start gearing yourself now, because if you are the kind of person that does not like stress, it is coming! If you don't like confrontation, get ready for it, because it is going to happen.

2ᴺᴰ Step: Give Them a Vision

The next thing that Moses did is he gave the people a vision for the future, but the vision could not come until they let go of the old system first. We know the people need a vision, but before they can receive the new vision, the old must be taken away. That is why you have to expose the system and shatter it.

You have to say, "You see this vision that you thought was so wonderful? It is false. It is wrong. It is a facade!"

Don't think that the people don't have a vision right now. They have a vision alright - of a couple of slave drivers whipping them and making them work. They have a vision like in the days of the Pharisees that says, "If I fast and pray long enough and worship hard enough, maybe God will accept me."

"If I sacrifice enough, somehow, I can enter into the presence of God."

"I cannot hear from God for myself, I have to go to the prophet to hear on my behalf."

That is the vision that they had. Don't think people don't have a vision. They have a clear idea in their minds of what it means to serve God.

Unfortunately, it is the wrong vision. Before you can give them the new one, you have to destroy the old one. Once you expose that vision for the fallacy that it is, you can step in and say, "Here's the land of milk and honey."

Jesus could step in and say, "I'm bringing the Kingdom a message of grace, a message of love and forgiveness to the sinners."

Why do you think prostitutes and all those sinners came back to Jesus? Because they took one look at the Pharisees and thought, "Forget it. I won't even get halfway to where they are! I don't match up, and I know I'm going to fail. I know I am going to sin. There's no way I will be as wonderful as that great man or woman of God.

"You know, I may as well pack it in now. There's no way I'll reach that! Besides, he's favored of the Lord. What does the Lord think about me? I'm not favored. He's the favorite one! God speaks to him."

CHANGE THEIR VISION

Jesus brought the Kingdom right down to the common man.

He said, "No, God speaks to you."

He started changing their vision, and He started bringing God to the people. God was no longer wrapped up in their phylacteries and their impressive garments. God was in their hearts. He was in their presence and in their lives. He was interested in knowing about their everyday circumstances.

Jesus was right there with the people, and He started giving them a vision and an illustration of what God was really like. That is the vision we will bring to God's people.

We are meant to be saying, "It's not about God's man for the hour. It's not about the big name or the holier-than-thou attitude. Being a Christian is about real life - daily living. It is about having God in every area of your life, in every breath of your lungs. It is having Him walking with you, talking with you, and this relationship is not just for the great names and the women and men of God behind the pulpit. It is for you - for every believer!"

"Do you know that you can hear from Him? Do you know that you have a ministry and can work for Him, and you are just as favored as anybody who is standing up there?"

That is the vision we are going to give the people of God.

We will say, "You know that anointing where only a select few are chosen to receive it? Well, every believer is one of the "select few." You see these great signs and wonders? It is your birthright. It is for you, little nobody that nobody looks sideways at, sitting in the pews at the back of the church.

"You mom, who has four kids hanging on her skirt, and all she ever does is cook, clean, and wash hair - it is your birthright to have the power of the living God dwelling in you, and around you, changing this world."

Most people though think, "Me? I'm not going to change the world. That's for the big names to do!"

Offer Something Better

No, it is for you. You must bring this message to His people. You have to give them a new vision. That is what Moses and Jesus did. They gave the people a new vision.

Moses said, "Guys, I have a land of milk and honey. You have no idea how wonderful it is going to be!"

Now they had something to aim towards. When they had something to aim towards, they were only too willing to let go of the old.

You see, you don't have to try and force people to let go of the old.

It's like this. If a child is holding the blade of a knife, you don't rip the knife out of the child's hand. You just offer it a candy. It will drop the knife straight away.

How Not to Do It

You can't go into a church and start telling the people, "Let go of this! Stop doing that. You need to get rid of how you teach and have more praise and worship. Throw away the programs, and add a new songbook."

What are you replacing it with? You want to rip away everything, but what are you giving them? Are you giving them something that is worth throwing the old out for?

You will not need to take anything out of the church. Just give them something new, and they will drop the old. They are not that foolish that they are going to hold onto something less beautiful. They will not hold onto a knife if they can have the candy. Give them some candy for a change.

> *The Lord didn't attack the sheep. He attacked the Pharisees. We sometimes get that mixed up.*

Not once did Jesus ever speak against the prostitutes or a tax collector! He spoke against the Pharisees.

You need to get that straight. You are not called to tear God's people apart and to rip everything out of their lives. You are called to give them a new vision, and a new goal, and then they will leave the old.

CHAPTER 14

THE SLAVERY MENTALITY

Chapter 14 – The Slavery Mentality

Once the vision was received by the children of Israel, the journey could begin. However, like any great vision, you discover why God's people are not yet walking in the Promised Land.

There are some things that hinder them from getting there. And so, as you start walking out your calling, you will come face to face with something I call, "The Slavery Mentality", in God's people.

On onward with all gusto, the system was exposed, and a vision given.

From there, let's take a good look at the Israelites going through the wilderness. They had finally left Egypt. The Lord had parted the Red Sea. It was glorious! There were miracles after miracles.

Fast forward to just one month later, and they didn't have anything to eat.... Their cry to Moses? "Let's go back to Egypt!"

They were hardly out of Egypt, and they were already wanting to go back.

Why was it like this? They had a slavery mentality. That is all they ever knew. They only knew how to be slaves and think like slaves. They couldn't think like leaders. They could not think like God's chosen people because from birth they had been trained, formed, and shaped to think like slaves.

They had templates built into them from years of people saying, "You're a slave. You're beneath the master."

And every time something went wrong, they wanted to run back to Egypt again, back to where they were comfortable. It was the slavery mentality that drove them there.

You are going to have to deal with that in God's people. They are bound with a mentality of slavery. They are bound with religion and rules, and it is the way they think. They are not even aware of it because it is all they know. They don't know any different.

The teacher is called to deal with templates and mindsets in God's people by the Word, to smash them and replace them. This is the primary function of the Moses apostle - to smash that mentality.

God's people think in bondage. They do not think, "I am called of God to stand up in this world, to shine, and be an example. I am a King's kid! I have an inheritance."

Christians do not think like that. Christians cower to the world. The Government barks, and they jump. Their boss barks, and they say, "How high?"

Now, I am not talking about rebelling against the government. I am talking about a mentality here. I am talking about being fearful and being controlled by the system. People are so used to being controlled by that system that they don't know any better. They have lost their independent thinking.

They have lost the revelation because they have been programmed to think, "This is the guy who's in charge, and you're lucky if you can even get to speak to him!"

They think, "So, who am I?"

A Swing to Domination

I tell you what - a slavery mentality also goes on the opposite end of the pendulum. You can have a person who has been oppressed continually and breaks free of that finally to start a new life. Unfortunately, if they do not deal with that mentality in themselves, they now want to rise up and dominate those who dominated them.

You have seen this, I'm sure. People with a slavery mentality go two ways. They either cower and always submit in fear, time and time again, and run back, or they rise up in their own strength and say, "I'm going to get that pastor back! I am going to show him! It is not good enough to break away. No, I have to show him who I am. I have to show him what I've got. I'm going to rise up and stand on his neck."

It is still a slavery mentality. I don't care how you rise up! I don't care how bold and confident you become in yourself. It is still a slavery mentality, and it is controlling you and God's people.

You see, Moses has to bring balance. On the one hand, you have to say, "Rise up! Know who you are. See who you are. Don't you realize that this is what you have, and this is what God's given you? This is your right and your authority."

On the other hand, he has to prevent them from going overboard.

You have seen this in Jesus' disciples. They never got it! Even after Jesus resurrected, they said, "Lord, are you now going to restore the kingdom to Israel?" (Acts 1:6)

I can just imagine Jesus going, "Oh man, it's been three years, guys. Come on, give me a break here!"

They had a slavery mentality. The disciples had a slavery mentality because of the Romans. The Romans had oppressed them. They had kept them under their thumbs with all their rules and regulations. So, the only way they could see through this was to rise up and conquer the Romans, to take the throne, and to restore David to the throne.

It was a slavery mentality though, and it prevented them from seeing the real reason why Jesus came to them in the first place. He didn't come to conquer Rome. He came to conquer the world, but not in the way that they thought.

You see, that thinking colored the way that they should have been thinking. They did not see the big picture. They were so restricted in their tunnel vision.

You, as a Moses apostle, have to show them the full picture. That means you had better be getting revelation from God, before you open your mouth. You had better make sure that you are saying the right things.

BE SPIRIT LED

You must also be confident. Once you have that mandate, you must be confident. You speak by the power of the Holy Spirit, and those templates will be smashed!

Don't think you can stand up and just talk because you have a conviction. It is not good enough to just have a conviction. What you say must be anointed by the Holy Spirit, so that it is a sword that divides the joints and the marrow and hits them between the eyes when you speak.

You have to speak under the anointing of the Holy Spirit. I just can't believe how many people overlook this. You can be a good teacher.

> ***You can speak good words, but unless you have the Holy Spirit standing behind you, your words are nothing! They will fall empty to the ground.***

However, if you speak under that anointing, it doesn't even matter what you say. You don't have to be eloquent and use all the right words. It really doesn't matter if you stutter. The Lord used fishermen and tax collectors. We are beyond that. If He can use them, He can use us. The important thing is to speak by the Spirit!

If there is one thing I can stress, even if you are a prophet, speak by the Spirit, not by yourself. If you speak by the Spirit, you will bring change. If you speak by yourself, your words will tickle some ears and fall to the ground.

Moses tried it in his own strength, and then he tried it in God's strength. When he tried it in God's strength, the whole of Israel listened, and the whole of Egypt trembled!

We have that same power within us. Moses had it in a rod. We have it in our spirits - that same power that parted the Sea. That same power that brought Egypt to its knees is dwelling inside each and every one of us.

It is about time we use a little of that, but we are doing everything with our heads. We are doing everything with our own mindsets, and our own preconceived ideas, instead of speaking with our spirits.

You need to speak from your heart. When you open your mouth, judge yourself. When you stand up and are ministering, are you speaking from your head, or are you speaking from your spirit? The Word says that we will be judged for every idle word. (Matt 12:36)

Do you have the confidence to stand and say, "Okay Lord, judge me. Judge the words that are coming out of my mouth,"? You are talking to His Bride.

You had better make sure that the words that are coming out are His words and not yours, because you are talking to His Bride. He is jealous of her. It is a tremendous responsibility.

REMOVE THE IDOLS

The next thing the Moses apostle will be called to do is to remove the idols. This one is tough! Moses didn't accomplish this completely.

Stephen says in Acts 7, "Oh yeah, you were so wonderful - the great big nation of God that took along with you all of your idols of Moloch and Baal and the rest of them. You carried them from Egypt with you into the desert and brought them with you to the Promised Land." (Acts 7:41-43)

Didn't they return back to idol worship time and time again? I believe that the idols are the most difficult thing to remove from a rebellious generation, and the main reason is because they do not know that they are idols.

Once again it is a mindset. People don't know that they are idols. To them, it is a way of life. The Israelites grew up in that society in the Egyptian heritage. They were really brought up as Egyptians. They had lost their identity when they became slaves, and so they worshipped the same gods that the Egyptians worshipped.

We look at them and say, "How stupid! Couldn't they see it's an idol?"

No, they actually couldn't see it. You read through the whole of the Old Testament, and you think, "These Israelites were a bunch of idiots! I mean, how difficult is it to understand, "Put no other gods before me."?

That is not such a hard commandment to follow, and yet, they built calves and a host of other idols and worshipped them. You see, they really did not see them as idols. To them, Lord Yahweh was trapped in the idol, and that is what they were worshipping.

SOMETHING TO SEE AND TOUCH

When they said to Aaron, "Put up a god," they did it because they were used to having something that they could visualize. It was not like today where we have the Holy Spirit with us, where we can close our eyes, and He is there. They needed something visual to fix their eyes on.

They said, "Okay, this is God. We can worship Him."

They were very visual people, and up until then, Moses was their icon. They knew that God was with Moses. When they fixed their eyes on Moses, that was okay. But now, Moses had gone, and they started losing touch.

They said, "We need something to fix our eyes on." So they said, "Build us a calf. That can be our god. God can be here."

Hasn't the Catholic Church done the same thing? If you read the history of the church, that is how it actually started coming in. People needed something visual to help connect them with worship.

They couldn't get into the Spirit because they had lost the gifts of the Spirit. They had also lost the anointing, so they needed something visual to help bring and connect them into the presence of the Lord. That is how it all started.

What happened though? Those visual aids started becoming idols, and before you knew it, it was part of their lives. They didn't see anything wrong with it. It seemed fine to them, but it was idolatry.

Traveling in Europe displayed this for me so graphically. Walking into churches hundreds of years old, sporting relics and the tombs of saints as a "point of contact" to the Lord. Light a candle, pray to the saint, and bow at his shrine. And this is called Christianity...

You know, don't think we are so different from the Catholics sometimes. We have our idols. We have our gods. How about materialism? You do not need to look far to see it.

Idol: Financial Prosperity

What is an idol except the thing that dictates the direction of your life and gains your worship before God does?

You say, "I will do anything except this one thing, Lord. You can have my life, but not my bank account. You can even have my house, but not my bank account."

Or perhaps, "You can have my bank account because it is empty, but the house is mine!"

(If you are a prophet, then your bank account is likely empty.) Isn't that true? These are idols that are worshipped.

I was watching a bit of TV, and you know, I am not very familiar with the election process here in the US. Where I come from, it is really not as much of an issue as it is here in America, so it is not really shown on TV quite as much. So, when I came here, and they were having elections, there was something new every time I turned it on. I was amazed.

The one great insult that one of the debaters brought in was, "Do you know that he's going to throw the financial stability of America?"

That would be unpardonable! Not our financial stability - anything but that! There goes the golden calf, and we bow down and worship the golden calf.

You say, "God supplied this calf to us. Let's worship it."

We have to reassess our lives. We have to start looking and seeing what our priorities are. Where do your priorities lie?

I am not saying that financial stability is a bad thing. I believe that every believer should be walking in financial prosperity. I believe that we should be walking in abundance and should be an example to this world.

> ***God is not going to give financial prosperity to the Church until they let that prosperity go first.***

God wants us to be a city that is set on a hill, so that the rest of the world can look at us and say, "I want what they have!"

He wants us to look good. He wants us to be prosperous, but He is not going to give it to us until we let it go. He will give it to us when it is not important to us because He can then trust us with it.

If He had to pour out financial prosperity on the churches right now, what do you think would happen? Take a look around you at where it has happened.

Every prophet has prophesied how a great abundance is going to be poured out on the Church, and I believe it. I believe that the kingdom of God is going to have all the wealth of the wicked. Why do you think it hasn't happened yet? It is because they are still too dependent on it.

Until we learn to let these idols go, the Lord will not give it to us. Don't think the Lord is trying to do the Church out of a blessing.

He is not. If we stay dependent on money for everything, it will ruin the body of Christ! If the Lord had to suddenly release all the finances He has promised for the church of God, they would only go one way, and I promise… it will not be to the Throne Room to worship. It will be the mall to blow it. That is why He has had to withhold it.

IDOL: GOVERNMENT

Then there is the issue of dependence on government, and the fear of the government. People look up to the government leaders for everything they do and say. This has been a tremendous debate, and I have gotten into some really touchy arguments with this one with many people.

People say, "If we're going to bring change in the Church, we have to bring it to our government first."

That is nonsense! Where does change take place? It takes place in the hearts of the men and women of God. Change does not take place in the mind. You cannot change people by changing their minds. You change people by changing their hearts, and their minds will change accordingly.

If you think you are going to bring change to the Church by standing up and spending all your money on government elections, and trying to get a seat in the Senate, forget it. It will not work! All you will be doing is grabbing for power. Let's get real.

You think you are doing it for the kingdom of God, but you are really standing up there because you are exalted, and everybody looks up to you. It is a position. Do you want to change the Church in your country? Start changing the hearts of God's people first. Let God position you in government later (if that is even what He wants). Prophets, you need to decree it. Apostles, you need to confront and bring down the plagues of Egypt.

Let's get away from doing it the world's way. You see, it is a mindset. It is that slavery mentality again, because that is all you know. We want to bring God back into the schools so we have to go to court.

No! Revive the heart of every youth you can get your hands on, and you will bring God back into the schools. Heaven help anybody who stops them from bringing God back into the schools, because they will be so on fire that people will not be able to stay away from them.

You are not going to bring God back into the schools by making it a law. You are going to bring God back into the schools by putting Him in the hearts of every child that goes to school. You are wasting your time, and you are wasting your money. Change the hearts of God's people. That is what He has called you to do.

Logical Reasoning is Useless

Jesus had the ability to stand up and speak with the best of them. He could talk the talk. Jesus could stand in a group of Pharisees and not flinch! He knew the Law better than they did, but He didn't run for office. Neither did any of the disciples. Yet, they birthed the New Testament church that moved in power.

The Word says the people were so afraid even to be associated with the early times apostles because of the power that came from their shadows. If you want to change this world, start with you, and you will start changing everybody else around you. You are not going to change this world by trying to change their minds. You can talk and argue for hours, but they will not get it. It doesn't come by logic.

> *How does salvation come? Salvation comes by conviction. You cannot speak conviction into somebody's head. Conviction comes from the heart.*

You were saved by a move of the Spirit and by conviction. What makes you think now that you will get the body of Christ to rise up and move to where they want to go by trying to fill their heads with a whole lot of words?

No, you have to bring that conviction again. You have to put new fire in their hearts, a new burden and a new passion. Then, you just let them loose a bit, and they will spread the fire. As I said, it starts today with you and me.

As I was preparing this chapter, the Lord brought an aspect to me that I had not considered before. Moses failed in breaking that slavery mentality of the children of Israel, and they didn't enter the Promised Land. He could not get it out of them. I daresay that, in the older generation of today, there will be very few who will enter into the new move of God.

There will be the Joshuas and Calebs, and that is why Moses has his work cut out for him. That is also why the Moses apostle has such a short time to work in. He is called to a stiff-necked generation that is not going to change.

It is like when the Lord said to Jeremiah, "Jeremiah, I have wonderful words for you to speak."

He said, "Yes!"

The Lord said, "The people aren't going to listen to them."

"Oh dear. I knew there was a catch!"

That is what the Moses apostle is called to do.

The Lord says, "I have raised you up for such a time as this. I have called you."

You say, "Oh wonderful, I'm a great apostle."

"They're not going to listen to you though."

You say, "Couldn't I just be a David, Lord?"

They are not going to listen, but you have been called to speak the word. Out of that, you will birth a new generation. You will preach and teach and train, and through it all, you will do something you did not expect.

You will see born, before your very eyes, a new generation. I was surprised when God did this to me. I have been working with leaders since I entered ministry. But, as the Lord started bringing us team members and spiritual sons and daughters, they were born from a new generation. Some of my spiritual children joined us through their parents who had enrolled in one of our schools! Talk about living a type and a shadow.

At first, I was not sure about it all – yet each way Craig and I turned, the Lord was bringing us a new generation of mighty warriors. Many were born out of the church system. All of them weary of the church system. All of them ready to take the Promised Land God's way.

You too will discover along this journey, as you push through with so many, that the secret mandate you have had all along has been to raise up the next generation!

CHAPTER 15

THE NEW GENERATION

Chapter 15 – The New Generation

The Lord has given me very clear revelation on the fact that there is going to be an influx of souls to the kingdom of God. They will come in these years like we have not seen in times past, nor will we see ever again.

The Lord is raising up from this rebellious, teenage generation, a new generation. It is a generation that does not have a slavery mentality, and is not bound by religion and the status quo thinking. This is the generation that we are going to be working with.

From the time that they are born again, God will put the correct pattern into them. Then, we are going to see a couple of gladiators arising. There is coming a harvest of souls into the kingdom of God that is going to blow us away. It will be a quick work because they are eager.

They are already rebelling against the system. You just point them in the right direction and let them go, and you have an army of Saul of Tarsus's on your hands.

As rebellious as Saul was, he was passionate and zealous! All the Lord did was pick Saul up and put him on the other road, and he kept on running. He was going in the opposite direction, but now, on the right road, he carried on with the same zeal.

That is what is going to happen with the new generation. I firmly believe in the youth of today. You look at them and think, "Oh Lord, what has happened to the generation of today? The music, the hairstyles, the clothing - they're more decadent than they've ever been before!"

Praise the Lord! They are so decadent because they are so rebellious against the system and because God is going to use it for His glory. What the devil thought was evil, God is going to turn to good.

The devil thought, "Yeah, I'll mess the Church around. I'll raise up a youthful generation that is full of it."

God said, "Go ahead. Make my day, because you won't see what I will do with them when I'm through!"

GET A NEW FIRE GOING

We are going to take that bunch of misfits, and we are going to have a revolution. The kingdom of God will have fire.

You want to make a fire? Get yourself a couple of really hot coals. Then, add some dead ones. Don't try and make a fire with just dead coals.

Sad fact for Moses though, you are called to make a fire with dead coals first. The good news? There will be some new ones too. In fact, there will be a lot of new ones. Once you have exhausted yourself on the old, the new will come.

The new generation did come, and they went through with Joshua into the Promised Land. You, as a Moses, are called to prepare the hearts of the people. You are not called to take them into the land. You are called to change their mindsets.

You see, that is why the Moses apostles are primarily teachers. It is because only a teacher, speaking by the Word, can speak as that two-edged sword, to smash the old and to give them the new.

The prophets have their place too. We will discuss that more later on. The Moses apostle is primarily a teacher because he has to use the Word of God to change the old way of thinking and to steer them into the right direction.

He just sets things up for Joshua to come and take them into the Promised Land. The Moses does not actually take them through. He prepares their hearts and minds and gets them ready. That is what you are called to do.

Signs and Wonders

I was also fascinated to see how much the Moses apostle functions in signs and wonders. In this day and age, we have signs and wonders, and they are a big thing. They always have been.

The idea of signs and wonders is magnificent, and you think, "Wow, that God would come down like He did on the day of Moses and part the Red Sea, slaughter the Egyptians, and do all that stuff! Man, if only we could see it, but God is refraining Himself. Only if we're lucky, or really good, will He come down and give us a couple of signs and wonders that can blow us away."

As I was meditating on this, the Lord said to me very clearly,

"Did you know that if it were up to me, there would be signs and wonders following every single believer every day of their lives? That it would be so common place you wouldn't even think about it anymore!

But, my people restrict me with their mindsets. They have such a naturalistic way of thinking that they can't see beyond it. They can't think in the supernatural because they are always thinking in the natural. They can't see in the Spirit because they are always looking in the world."

He said, "Oh that my people would just see what I see, that they would just give me a chance, and let me at it! I would turn this world upside down through my people. There would be signs and wonders following every believer."

What is the mindset? The mindset is, "To operate in signs and wonders, you have to be specially anointed and released. You need to go to Bible School, and then you have it. That is what it is."

"You need a lot of faith. God can do it, but He will not use me because I have not earned the right yet. I have not got the formula for it."

"With all my knowledge, I see just how big the miracle has to be to bring this healing, and the mountain of evidence is bigger than the off chance we will see a miracle."

Truth: Every single believer has the Holy Spirit dwelling within them. Every believer has the ability to have signs and wonders in their shadow, just like Peter did. Unfortunately, they don't want it badly enough.

EARNESTLY DESIRE THEM

The Lord is not going to shove something at you and say, "Here!"

You have to ask for it first. What does the Word say? It says that we should earnestly desire spiritual gifts and earnestly hunger after them (1 Cor 14:1). Well, the people of God don't know that they are allowed to hunger for them. What have they been taught to do?

"Sit down, shut up, and when I give you a chance, you can talk. Certainly don't desire anything, because I'm the one with the answers."

No. We have to teach God's people to desire, which means we have to desire it ourselves so passionately that we have to hunger for it! We have to thirst for it, and then we have to impart a bit of that hunger and thirst to them.

You can't say, "Lord, that church needs revival badly!"

What about you? How is your heart looking before God? Are you hungry enough? Are you desiring enough and thirsting enough? Is the fire burning so much in your belly that you lie awake at night saying, "Lord, I've got to have more! You've got to do something. Lord, I'm just not satisfied. I want more. It's not enough. I don't want double. I want triple!"

Are you greedy enough to hunger after the Holy Spirit like that? Once you are, you get around somebody like that, and it is contagious! You want to be around them. The more they talk, and the more they hunger, you find your own spirit being stirred up, don't you?

Why not be that fire? You just can't help yourself when people are around you. You will hunger, and thirst, and you will share with them. You will just be talking, and they will say, "Man, that sounds good!"

Paint Good Pictures

Are you making people hunger and thirst? Are you hungry and thirsty yourself? Because, until you are, you have nothing to give them. You will just be giving them a bunch of dead works. You have to be hungry and thirsty, and then you have to serve it up.

That is what the Moses apostle does. He prepares a gourmet meal, and he serves it up for them. They go, "Ooh, I can't wait to dig in!"

When this happens, you will be fighting the people off and saying, "Give me a break, guys. I have to get some rest!"

Right now, you are probably saying, "What are you doing? Don't go. Come back!"

They are gone though. They don't want to know your problems. Give them something that they want and desire, and you will see the body of Christ rise up in a way that we have never seen it rise up before. It starts with us.

Fresh Revelation

In conclusion, I want to end on this one point. It is that you must receive fresh revelation all the time, particularly if you are called to be a Moses apostle. If you are to teach God's people, receive fresh revelation daily. You don't feed somebody week-old bread. That means that you are on your face before God all the time.

You see, you might think that you have it made. You might think, "Well, this Word smashes that template, and that Word hits that mindset."

Forget it. Everybody is different. Every congregation is different, which means that you need a fresh word every time. That means if you are to be hitting the mark first time, without exhausting yourself, you need to get fresh revelation.

The prophets have heard me say this often. They are carrying on and on, and I say, "Hang on a minute guys. Get revelation!"

Getting revelation is so important, and so simple, but we overlook it. We think because we have the knowledge of the Word and the knowledge of experience in ministry and life that we can just stand up any time we want to and just speak. It comes back to speaking from our spirits.

Take the Word of God, combine it with the revelation of the Spirit, and you have a bullet that is going to hit the heart of man first time, every time! That word will bear fruit and bring change. If you are just speaking words, it is going to bounce off.

There needs to come a balance. You have to know the Word. Prophecy is not enough. The Lord gave us Genesis to Revelation for a reason. You must use it. But, when you apply the revelation of the Spirit to that Word and speak, you change lives.

Make your words count! When you say something, instead of just babbling away, make them count. If you meet somebody for the first time, do they go away remembering what you said. Do they go away thinking, "I never thought of that before!"?

Did you paint a picture? Did you give a concept or do anything to change that person's heart?

Get revelation. Change the hearts of God's people everywhere you go, and everywhere you speak. Make it part of your daily walk. Even when you speak at work, you don't necessarily need to throw a Scripture at them. Just make sure that what you say is by the Spirit of God.

They said of Jesus, "Never a man spoke as this man," and these were the Roman legionaries. Nobody ever spoke like Him. Ungodly men respected Jesus. Ungodly men looked at Him and said, "Wow. That meant something!"

Are even the people in your workplace saying that about you?

Are you speaking words, not even necessarily Scripture, but the kind of words that are hitting them between the eyes, and that are changing their hearts? That is what we are called to do.

We are called to start with our hearts, and then we are called to influence those around us. As God raises up the Moses apostles and puts them in charge of His people, they are called to stand in front of the masses and say, "Thus saith the Lord, we're going to the Promised Land, and this is how we're going to do it."

Are you prepared to stand up today as a leader and say, "Okay Lord, I can't imagine this will be fun… but let's do it."? Then you are ready. Get equipped because you are about to change the Church!

CHAPTER 16

BOOT CAMP: HOW MOSES IS TRAINED

Chapter 16 – Boot Camp: How Moses is Trained

At this stage of the journey, you have dealt with Pharaoh. You have gone through the wilderness yourself, and you have climbed the mountain. You have confronted Pharaoh and all the obstacles that stood between you and the call on your life. You have gone back into the system, and you have gone on to be effective for the Lord.

Now comes the most exciting part of your journey! This is where you begin leading the children of Israel out of the bondage of slavery that they are in, into victory and into the Promised Land.

We start off this chapter in Exodus 19:3 to 5, speaking of the children of Israel:

> *And Moses went up to God, and the Lord called to him from the mountain, saying, "Thus you shall say to the house of Jacob, and tell the children of Israel:*
>
> *4 'You have seen what I did to the Egyptians, and how I bore you on eagles' wings and brought you to Myself.*
>
> *5 Now therefore, if you will indeed obey My voice and keep My covenant, then you shall be a special treasure to Me above all people; for all the earth is Mine.*

A Glimmer of Hope

How exciting! Moses was eventually beginning to see some of the fruit and some of the promises that the Lord had given him all along this journey. Things were starting to take place. Before, what was a glimpse of hope or a glimmer of expectation was now starting to unfold before him.

The children of Israel *did* listen! They did receive his message! Not only that, but they were excited and stood with him. They believed that he spoke for God. It was right there. The Promised Land was not far away. He could see the end was right there in his grasp. It was in sight.

Here the Lord was saying, "If only you just keep my commandments, I am going to lead you to the Promised Land. Not only am I going to lead you there, but I will also raise you up and make you greater than any other people!"

I can imagine Moses was really excited. I can imagine how he must have felt receiving that message from the Lord and looking down at the people and saying, "We did it! I can't believe it. We actually did it. We are not in Egypt anymore."

At this stage, the Red Sea had drowned the Egyptians, and here he was. The promise was right in front of him.

Leadership Training Begins

Now, we start looking at a deeper training that Moses had to go through, because he still had a couple of rough edges. The Lord had dealt with a lot of things that were inside Moses. He had dealt with his templates, his fears, and his bad image. There was something else that Moses had to come to terms with and overcome. That was his ability as a leader.

It wasn't just enough to overcome his fears. It wasn't just enough for him to realize, "Hey, these weaknesses are dealt with."

Now, it was time for the Lord to begin building on the foundation, to start raising him up as a mighty leader. The negatives had been removed, but now the positive needed to be added to make Moses the leader that God wanted him to be.

Intense Preparation for a Greater Ministry

The training of a Moses apostle is one on the move so to speak. Moses doesn't stay in the background and get to test his wings out on just a few people like David did in the Cave of Adullam. I think David had it a little easier. He had his mighty men in the

Cave of Adullam. If he made a mistake, it wasn't such an issue because it was just a few guys.

It wasn't like that with Moses though. It was all or nothing with him. He had the entire nation of Israel under him! One mistake affected all of them. He was trained on the move, and that is why he had to go through such a long period of preparation. The Lord had to make sure that he wouldn't make those mistakes, because it literally affected millions of lives.

So is the case for you as a Moses apostle. That is why your preparation has been so intense. That is why you have been out of the system for so long, and why it seems like everything has been pulled out of you time and time again.

You have looked around you, and you have seen others younger than yourself rise up quickly and go on with their ministry. You have watched them go on to be famous and successful, and here you are still sitting wondering, "When is it going to start for me Lord? Why are they going ahead? Why is everything moving for them, and I never seem to go anywhere?"

That is because when you finally do rise up, you will not rise up on a small scale. You see, David had a transition. He had little tastes of leadership until he was finally the leader of the whole of Israel. Moses went from all to nothing, and then, from nothing to all.

There wasn't any in between with Moses. No. He went from being a leader of nothing to being a leader of the entire nation of Israel. He went from having no experience to leading groups.

All he led at the beginning was a bunch of sheep, and that doesn't take much effort. They don't shout back. They do not complain. He went from that to leading millions of people.

That is why his preparation was so long, because he came into confrontation with the masses. He deals with the masses, with the big groups, and with the system. He works within the system, and he cannot afford to make the same mistakes that those who went before him made.

He cannot afford to lead the children of Israel back into slavery instead of the Promised Land. That is why his preparation and training phase is so long. So, be encouraged if you seem to be bordering on fifty years old and you are still wondering when your ministry will begin. It is because God has prepared you for something greater and more magnificent!

Jesus was trained His entire life for just three years of ministry. Look at what He accomplished in just three short years! He laid a foundation for the entire Church. The same goes for Moses.

You may not burn brightly for as many years as others, but for the time that you burn, you are going to make a powerful impact on the body of Christ. You may have been trained for longer, but your impact will be stronger and more magnificent than those who have gone before you.

SUDDENLY VISIBLE

So, if it seems as though you have been in the wilderness forever, be encouraged! This is because when you start working with the body of Christ, it will be a quick and a powerful work! You will see immediate fruit to all the preparation you have been through for so many years.

It will seem as though you have just risen up overnight, and people will say, "Wow, where did you come from? You came from nowhere."

Little did they know that you were being birthed in the bowels of the earth, through fire and travail and burning! You were being birthed over a period of time to qualify you to rise up suddenly into the light.

People will not see that. They won't see the travail and the burning. All they will see is this bright, big, building springing up in front of them. All they will see is Moses standing up before the masses and parting the Red Sea. You will go from nothing right up to everything in the blink of an eye. By one move of His hand, it will happen, and it will be miraculous.

It will not be because of your doing, because of your ability, or because of your strength. It will be because of His grace, and His calling and anointing on your life.

He is the one who has prepared you and trained you. He is the one who will continue to train you as you take the people of God that He has brought to you, and begin now taking them with you to the Promised Land.

Failure Through Disobedience

That is not what happened though, is it? It didn't work out that way. Moses didn't take the people to the Promised Land. What is the first thing that happened? In Numbers 14:33-34, God says to the children of Israel:

> *And your sons shall be shepherds in the wilderness forty years, and bear the brunt of your infidelity, until your carcasses are consumed in the wilderness.*
>
> *34 According to the number of the days in which you spied out the land, forty days, for each day you shall bear your guilt one year, namely forty years, and you shall know My rejection.*

God had said to them beforehand, "If you will indeed obey my voice and keep my Covenant, then you shall be a peculiar treasure and above all people."

What did the children of Israel do? The first sight of the Promised Land, and they trembled and said, "We can't do this. Forget it! We can't take this land," and they broke God's promise.

He said, "Because you broke my promise, you will wander in the wilderness for forty years - a year for each day that the spies had gone out."

IT STARTS WITH DEATH

So, apostle, the first phase of your training in leading the children of Israel from slavery to the Promised Land is a phase commonly known as death. Have you heard that word before?

You say, "I was excited! I had these expectations, and it was all coming together. People were accepting my ministry. My teaching was just getting out there, and then suddenly, right in the middle of it, it was like the brakes were put on. Everything came to a grinding halt! I could take the people so far and no further. They didn't want to hear the new revelation."

You wanted to keep moving them to the next stage. When you started out with them they were excited and said, "Hey, that's good. What you're sharing is good," and so, they grew with you.

It was so exciting! But then, you came up against a wall where you took a step, and they said, "We don't want to take that step with you."

You said, "Come on guys! Can't you see what the Lord is telling us?"

They said, "I don't know. I'm not ready to take that step. I don't want to take it."

There is resistance to change, and they say, "No, I am going so far and no further!"

Moses says, "Lord, you've called me to lead these people out. You've called me to tell them the truth, but they don't want to listen, Lord! I don't know what to do."

You try hard to convince them. You fast and pray, and God says to you, "Let them die!"

You say, "God, I poured so much time into these people! You sent them to me, didn't you?"

"Yes."

"So then, surely I must complete what you've told me to do."

"No, let them die."

You say, "Why Lord? Why must I let them die?"

The Moses apostle then has nothing else to hold onto but the Word of God. He has to believe that God has sent him. He will have nothing to hold onto - no excitement, no vision, no goal and ambition.

He will have nothing to hold onto except, "I know God has put me here! I know God's given me a job to do, and I'm just going to keep on being diligent to what He's given me to do.

"I don't understand why things are not working out as they should. I don't know why I'm struggling the way I am, but I know that I must keep on pushing through."

So, you have to die to your great expectations and your visions. You have to die to everybody you poured so much into, and you have to leave them behind.

You have to come to that place of saying, "Okay Lord, I failed."

You must die to your leadership ability, or in this case, your lack of leadership ability.

REALIZING YOUR FAILURE

I often say that when the Lord begins teaching you and training you to be a leader, do you want to know what the first lesson is you learn? You learn what a leader you are not!

> *The first thing you learn about becoming a leader is what a bad leader you really are.*

You learn how lousy you are, and that all the leadership ability you thought you had is actually quite pathetic. You see, you started becoming comfortable with this idea. People have been accepting you. You are getting out there, and they are accepting your teaching.

You are thinking, "I can do this! This is okay."

So, you start thinking, "Well, maybe I'm not such a bad leader after all. Maybe I can handle this bunch of people. Maybe I can do this thing."

That happens until a death comes, and the Lord says, "You think you're such a hotshot? You really think you are such a great leader. I hate to break it to you, but you are not such a great leader."

LEADERSHIP TRAINING

For you, your leadership is in God, and in Him alone. For as long as you are leaning on Him, your leadership will stand. As long as you are leaning on yourself, your leadership will fall.

Moses is the opposite to David. David was a strong natural leader. He could stand, and people would flock to him. Moses' leadership was in God alone. When Moses was speaking for God, the very earth shook! The mountain quaked, and the lightning bolts came down. When Moses spoke for himself, the people grumbled.

The Moses apostle can never afford to stand up and speak for himself. That is your limp, apostle. When you are just you, that is exactly what you are – just you! When you stand up to speak for just yourself, people will see what a leader you are not. They will see that the Lord has indeed taken a weak vessel and made it into something glorious.

That is what makes the Moses apostle unique, however, in that when he steps into the cloud of God's glory, that glory cloud covers him, and all the people see is Jesus. That is his strength and his weakness.

His strength is that he will get to enter into a face-to-face relationship with God like no other man. His weakness is that the minute he steps out of that, he will be nothing but a man.

That is his limp. Moses had to realize that, without God, and without the miracles and His power, he wasn't a leader. He was nothing. All he was, was a vessel to be used of God. If he wasn't being used of God, then he was an empty vessel.

Hunger for the Lord

You will live, and you will hunger for His anointing and His power twenty-four hours a day. You will never be satisfied until you have His continual anointing. The minute you stop wanting that and become complacent, that is the minute you will die.

This is because the Moses apostle is continually seeking and being passionate about being in God's presence all the time. He is continually filling up on it and consuming it. He never gets sick of it. He hungers for it, and he yearns for it. From the day he is born until the day he dies, he is continually passionate and wanting more and more of God.

Isn't this what Moses said to God? He said, "God, I want to see your face."

Until he saw God's face, he was saying, "I want to see your face. I want more. I want you, and I need you. Be with me. Stand with me."

In that is your strength. Without it, you are nothing. You are a weak man, and you will fall. Your ability and strength are in His power and in knowing Him and speaking to Him face-to-face.

Perhaps people even look at you and say, "What's with you that you can't be normal and have a normal conversation? You can't just hang out like the rest of us."

The Moses apostle doesn't have time to hang around. He does not have time for trivialities of life because he wants God. He wants everything about Him. He wants to taste Him and smell Him and feel Him and know Him. When he is standing in the cloud of God's glory, that is when he is standing as a Moses apostle, leading God's children from slavery to the Promised Land.

So, that is your limp, and your strength. It is your death and your resurrection, all in one. Your death is that your flesh will always be there. You will always be a weak man. That is the way God has made you.

He has made you like that so that you would continually hunger for Him and that you would never be satisfied. If God wanted the strong and able, they would not need His glory. He chose the weak and foolish, and that is why He chose you. He will continually pour His glory upon you.

For as long as you are weak and foolish, He will continually pour out His grace, His power, and His anointing upon you. When you become exalted in your own eyes and think that you have something to do with your ability, or something to do with this position that you have been put in, that is when you will be humbled and brought down to death.

It will be a death and a resurrection, a death and a resurrection. It will be the story of your life. The power and the change and the transformation that will come upon the Church because of your ministry is worth that price!

LEARNING TO LET GO

The greatest death that Moses had to face was stepping back. It says in Numbers 14:44:

> *But they presumed to go up to the mountaintop. Nevertheless, neither the ark of the covenant of the Lord nor Moses departed from the camp.*

This passage is about when the children of Israel realized, "Hang on, we've missed it!" They suddenly wanted to go back because now God had withdrawn His promise.

They said, "We'll go and take the Promised Land, and God will be with us."

Moses said, "Don't do it! God is not with you this time. You failed."

They said, "Oh, what does Moses know? We'll go ahead anyway."

So, the Ark of the Covenant and Moses stayed behind in the camp. It goes on to say in verse 45:

> *Then the Amalekites and the Canaanites who dwelt in that mountain came down and attacked them, and drove them back as far as Hormah*

Moses had to stand back, knowing very well that they would be wiped out.

SO FAR AND NO FURTHER

There has to come a time where you let go. The Lord will bring many to you, but there will be those that you can take so far and no further. We dealt a lot with this in "Handling a Rebellious Generation."

There will be those that you will succeed with. There will be those that you will be able to take a short part of the way, and some you will be able to take even further. There will only be a few that you will be able to take all the way.

You need to know when to let go and to let them go their way. You see, God never forces His will on any man, and He will not take them any further than they want to go. If He will not force His will on them, then you cannot force your will on them either. You have to come to the point of letting them go.

SOME TOUGH EXPERIENCES

This is something we have often experienced in our own ministry. The Lord has brought us people with such potential, and we have seen growth in them overnight! We have poured everything into them. We have ministered in love, counseled and taught them. We have raised them up by our very hands.

Then, they have come to a stage in their lives where they say, "So far and no further!"

You want to push them beyond and say, "Your goal is just over the next hill! If you just push a little more, you'll be there."

They say, "This is where I'm going, and I'm not moving from here!"

They come to a stage where they will not receive from you any longer. You try and try until eventually the Lord says, "Let them go!"

"Yes, but Lord, if I let them go and go the way they want to, they are going to be killed. The enemy is going to attack them. Lord, I know what's going to happen if we let them go."

He says, "It's their choice. You must let them go."

There have been stages in our ministry where whole groups of people who had been with us since the very beginning suddenly left, all at the same time.

We said, "Lord, what is going on?"

He said, "They will go so far and no further. They have become hardened and restrictive. I cannot do anything with them."

You took them as far as they were prepared to go, and you did well. But, it is time to let them go now. Has it even occurred to you that, in addition to their own choices, this was always what God intended? That this was as far as He always wanted you to take them?

I think that has to be the hardest death for the Moses apostle to face, knowing firstly that he has to let them go, and they will never go to the Promised Land. Even more painful is knowing that if they go the way they want to go, they are going to be destroyed by the enemy.

You know that there is nothing out there but pain, strife, and struggle, and that they will never reach the goal that they think is out there.

Too Great a Price

You see, the children of Israel thought they would really do it. They thought they would really conquer that land, but they found out too quickly that it was not to be. Moses knew it was going to happen, but he had to let them go.

Sometimes, there will be those that you know you have to let go of, and you know what is going to happen to them. You know that the enemy is going to attack them and that they will fall, but you have to step back.

You cannot force your will on them. You have done well. You have taken them as far as you could. Now, it is time for you to move on, and a lot of the time, you have to leave them behind.

You cannot stop growing just because they stop growing. This will happen for as long as you continually grow. This is what happened with Moses. He was continually changing, growing and being trained, and so, a transformation was taking place in his life all the time.

There was a progression. The Lord was giving more and more revelation with each stage that they went through, but the people came to a point and said, "That's it! We're not going any further. We are not prepared to face the giants. We're not prepared to pay the price."

You will say to those who are following you, "Guys, this is the promise the Lord has for us, but this is the price."

They will say, "I'm not prepared to pay that price."

> **Let them go and stand back. The children of Israel didn't want his answer. They didn't want His anointing. God could do nothing with them!**

There will be another test, followed by another resurrection. So, press on because the story isn't over yet.

THE UPRISING FROM WITHIN

Moses faced yet more tests. As if the death wasn't enough, or the devastation of not completing this goal that he had in his mind was not enough, he faced his greatest fear. Read from Numbers 16:3:

> *They gathered together against Moses and Aaron, and said to them, "You take too much upon yourselves, for all the congregation is holy, every one of them, and the Lord is among them. Why then do you exalt yourselves above the assembly of the Lord?"*

Do you know who was speaking here? It was Korah. He was part of the same tribe that Moses and Aaron came from. That is hitting a bit close to home. What was Moses' greatest fear when he first confronted Pharaoh? It was, "What if the people reject me? What if they say, 'Who sent you? God didn't send you.'"

Now, here he was. It was finally happening. His own people were saying, "Who do you think you are? Do you think you are the only one God can speak through?"

Moses couldn't run away. God was trying to put some strength into him. He was trying to put a bit of mettle into him, and He was saying, "I want you to face this Moses."

He was putting it right up in his face and saying, "I want you to face this - the last of your greatest fears. I want you to overcome now."

The same thing happened with Miriam and Aaron. Yet, again, he was faced with this conflict.

FACING YOUR FEARS

What are you going to do with it? What will happen when your greatest fear does really come upon you?

We spoke in "Confronting Pharaoh" about how you overcome the fear within. We spoke about how you face that fear in your own mind, and how when you go out, it is not so bad. But, here is the real thing - what happens if after all that, you really do come face-to-face with your greatest fear? How are you going to respond?

Are you going to justify yourself and say, "Hey, I did all the work. I didn't feel like leaving the wilderness anyway, but God's the one who appointed me. Really, I think I'm the best leader for the job. Can't you see what a good leader I am, and what wonderful leadership ability I have?"

Will you stand on your natural leadership skills and say, "Well I'm the boss around here!"?

Are you going to be a dominating leader that says, "Well, I'm the boss, and I get to say what goes on here. I don't care what you have to say."?

How are you going to respond to this test? How are you going to react when this happens to you? What did Moses do? Moses had learned that in himself he was but a mere man, but he had learned that when he stood in the cloud of God's glory, he stood in magnificence.

So, Moses opted for the magnificence. He opted to fall on his face in the middle of the cloud. God took him from his face and stood him on his feet. He put him right up there in the front, and it was God who vindicated him.

The resurrection came when Moses passed the test! You know, the Lord did not make it very easy for him. He really had to prove himself.

Rejection From Inner Circle

Let's have a quick look now at what happened with Miriam and Aaron. It says in Numbers 12:1-2:

> *Then Miriam and Aaron spoke against Moses because of the Ethiopian woman whom he had married; for he had married an Ethiopian woman.*
>
> *2 So they said, "Has the Lord indeed spoken only through Moses? Has He not spoken through us also?" And the Lord heard it.*

That sounds awfully familiar to the accusation we just read about. That is the same thing that Korah and his crowd said.

They said, "Do you think you're so holy? We're just as holy! We're also from the tribe of Levi. What makes you so holy, and you are the only one who is called of God?"

Here came the same accusation, but this accusation was even closer to him. This was his own brother and sister. Before, it was Aaron who had stood with him in the trial, and the only one who understood him. He was the one Moses leaned so heavily on in the beginning of this journey. He was closest to Aaron, and yet he rose up against him.

It is going to happen, apostle. There will come a time when even those closest to you are not going to understand what God is doing in your life. This is because He will be speaking to you face-to-face and giving you the revelation alone. The time will come when even they won't fully grasp what you are saying, and you will have nothing to stand on, nothing but His Word and His anointing.

Those attacks that come so close to you are the most painful and devastating. You can take people accusing you out there that don't know you. You can handle it because you say, "What do they know anyway?"

When those that know you and are close to you bring that accusation, it shakes you. It makes you doubt your call.

It makes you wonder, "Did I really hear from God? Am I missing this thing? Lord, if even they think I'm missing it, then maybe I am in deception here. Maybe I'm wrong."

WAIT FOR GOD'S VINDICATION

God didn't even wait for Moses to do anything this time. He said, "Moses, Aaron, Miriam, get here now!" and He called them to the tent.

He came down, and He said, "Who do you think you are, speaking to my servant Moses like this? I have put him in charge and in this position, and don't you dare raise your voice up against him!"

He struck Miriam down with leprosy, and Moses had to pray for her so that she would be healed again.

Moses did not say a word to them, nor did he say a single word in his defense. He just stood, and he waited. God moved on his behalf, because you see, Moses had learned to stand in the cloud. If those closest to you are rising up in accusation, you just need to wait. God will rattle their teeth well enough.

They have dedicated their lives to Him as well. They have also submitted to the call on their lives as you have submitted to the call on yours, and God is not going to leave it unattended to.

Wait for God to speak to them. It may not be such a pleasant word. It may not be what they want to hear. They may have to face a few deaths of their own. But, don't react. God will vindicate. If you react and act out of the flesh, you will just prove what they are accusing you of. Stand and see the salvation of the Lord.

You must realize that as His grace was extended to you, it will be extended to them also. They need to get the revelation for themselves, even if that revelation comes with a smack up the side of their head. Their revelation will come if you will stand back and let God be God.

If Moses had got in there to try and convince them and deal with it himself, he could have split the camp in half. Everybody would have been voting, "Who's going to lead us? Miriam, Aaron or Moses?"

He didn't do that. He stood and waited, and God spoke and vindicated. He gave the revelation in His time.

You have to trust God more than you trust in their ability to fail. You have to trust Him to speak to them because they have dedicated their lives to Him too. He is not going to leave them out in the wilderness. He is taking them with you.

Step back, keep quiet, and let Him speak, because He will. You may need to minister to them afterwards because they may have to go through some heavy deaths, but God will speak.

Visible Attack

Moses overcame one of his greatest fears – those closest to him rejecting him. He could face it, and he overcame it. God stood by him and it was okay. Then what happened? The next biggest fear. It says in Numbers 16:19:

> *And Korah gathered all the congregation against them at the door of the tabernacle of meeting. Then the glory of the Lord appeared to all the congregation.*

This guy went just a little bit too far. He didn't only get personal with Moses, but he went and gathered the entire congregation so that they could come and watch this!

Moses had said to them, "Okay guys. You don't think I'm the one that should lead you? All right, come and let's see what happens. Let's get together, and let God decide what should happen."

So, Korah tried to prove his point in public. He was so bold and confident in himself. He called everybody to come and watch it.

How many times has this happened in your ministry, where people have attacked you publicly have said, "I am going to cripple you."?

I can't tell you how many times I have had this myself.

People say, "That does it! I'm going to do everything in my power to see that your ministry is destroyed! You think you can treat me like this? You think you speak for God? Who do you think you are? You don't speak for God!"

Then, they go all out to totally discredit you publicly. They preach against you and speak against you. They write to others about you and forward emails about you to try and discredit your name. They get as many as they can on their side.

UNDERSTANDING AUTHORITY

Tell me now, how do you respond to that? How would you respond? Be honest. The first time you faced that situation you blew up in seven directions, all at once, justified yourself with every justification you could think of and started a war.

No, that is not the way to do it. That is not the way Moses did it. Moses had learned a thing or two. He said to Korah in Numbers 16:16:

> *And Moses said to Korah, "Tomorrow, you and all your company be present before the Lord—you and they, as well as Aaron.*

He got up in their face and said, "Hey you, you get here tomorrow at my command, and you had better listen to me!"

He didn't budge. He didn't make excuses for himself. He did not back down or tremble one bit! Moses had had enough. He had learned a little of how to be a leader.

He had overcome the fear in his own mind. So now, when he faced that fear, in reality, it was nothing. He had already overcome the greatest obstacles that were already in his head. Now, it was just a matter of working out what he had already faced in his wildest imagination and in his greatest fears.

He stood up to Korah who was such a strong leader, and here was little Moses who didn't even want to talk when God first called him. Now, he was standing up saying, "Listen, this is what you are to do. You do it now, and you do it when I want to do it. You get here!"

So, Korah brought all the congregation with him and thought, "Well, that'll show him. That'll teach him."

GOD'S FURY UNLEASHED

Moses had learned a thing or two, and what happened? If you follow the story, you will know that God got really mad!

He said, "I'm going to wipe out this whole congregation! They want to come and watch? They want to come and observe this spectacle of seeing Moses getting wiped out? Well, I have news for them. You want to come and watch this. I'm going to wipe the whole lot of you out!

He said, "There's just black or white. There are no in-betweens. You are on one side or the other. If you want to obey Korah's command, then you can't be very faithful to Moses anyway. So I'll wipe the whole lot of you, and Moses I'll just raise up a nation from you. It's not a problem. Let me just take the whole lot of them out."

Moses and Aaron had to say, "Hey Lord, that's not fair! You know Korah incited them. You can't take out the people because of a few men's sins."

So God calmed down a bit and was gracious, and He said, "Okay, congregation, you choose. Choose who is with Korah and who is with Moses. Pick your side. There are no gray areas. It is one or the other."

STAY IN THE CLOUD

When they had chosen their side, Korah and all those who stood with him were utterly destroyed! Everything was destroyed – their tents and all their possessions. There wasn't any in-between.

This was an incredible and mighty God that Moses knew and had on his side. But, you see, Moses had learned to stand in the cloud. Moses had learned that it was not his strength, but God's strength.

When you just stand in that cloud, that is really all you need to do. You don't need to talk. You don't need to justify yourself or make excuses. Just stand, and God will move on your behalf. But the minute you step out of that cloud, death will come.

You will be humbled again and again. Get back into that cloud, because, in yourself, you are nothing. In Him, they had better tremble and be very careful what they say to you. Not a single mouth was allowed to rise up against Moses, or God would deal with them! That is a really powerful position to be in.

Aaron's Rod

God was then gracious, and gave them a sign, showing that Aaron was indeed to be the Priest. They did the sign with the rods, and Aaron's rod budded. (Exodus 7)

God was once again confirming, "This is the line that I've called to be the priests. It's Moses that I have called to raise my people and take them into the Promised Land."

God continually confirmed Moses' leadership. He never got tired of it. He never forgot about Moses. You know, sometimes, we think that God forgets about us. We think that we need to take this whole thing into our own hands. We think that this is our ministry that we need to be in charge of.

We think that if we are not there to look after things and take care of the details, that it is going to fall apart. What you have done is stepped out of the cloud because you think it actually has something to do with you.

> *It is God's ministry, it is His calling, and they are His people.*

For as long as you just stand where He wants you to stand, He will work out the details, and He will confirm when He needs to confirm. He will move the cloud and the pillar of fire where He wants to move it.

Don't think you need to help Him along the way. He has everything in a perfect plan and pattern. Don't try and rush ahead of Him, and don't try and drag your feet. Just stand in His cloud, and go where He goes.

There is nothing very complicated about that, because when you are in the middle of that cloud, that is when the nations will tremble! That is when things will happen, and the change will come.

CHAPTER 17

THE FINAL REWARD

Chapter 17 – The Final Reward

As the Lord shifts and changes you through this process, it becomes difficult to remember the fire you started out with. It becomes dim at times through the attacks, rejection, and work at hand.

Between keeping everyone in line and blazing through the rejections and changes in direction, you forget that the Lord is not done with you just yet. In fact, when you feel the emptiest and have been stripped of every last bit of pride, He will come through with a promotion.

God's Gift to Moses

God gave Moses a new generation. There are those who left you in anger and those who the Lord removed because they rebelled. For every one of those, the Lord will raise up another one who is passionate and zealous and ready to go the distance.

We have seen this. We have been devastated at times in our ministry when the Lord seemed to do a culling.

He would just take out whole groups, and we would say, "Lord, you whittled us down to nothing here. What's happening?"

However, just as quickly, He would breathe in more fresh, zealous people who meant business with Him. He brought those who wanted to go that extra mile. They were young. They were passionate. They were ready for change, and they wanted to do whatever God required of them.

So, as they came in, we could pour everything into them that we had. Instead of them going so far and no further, they kept on going further. In fact, we had to keep running because they wanted more and more.

They started saying, "When's the next lecture coming out? When's the next move? What is the next step?"

We were saying, "Hey, I'm trying to finish up with this one!"

POSSIBILITY THINKING

There came a new generation, with a new way of thinking, and a new mentality. Moses took this new generation, and he began pouring into them everything he had.

When they came to the Promised Land the second time and sent in the spies, they all came back with that possibility thinking saying, "Yeah, we can do this! Come on guys, the land is magnificent! Just wait until you see it."

Moses had programmed God's way - all of them geared for success. The older generation didn't want to be re-programmed. They said, "We're sticking with our mindsets. We're sticking with our old templates, and that is that!"

In the new generation, Moses built those new templates. He poured into them. He changed them. He molded them, and they all became possibility thinkers like him. Upon them was built the new foundation that took the Promised Land.

Moses Apostle, God is going to bring you a new generation. For all those that you had to leave behind, let go, and die to, He is going to bring a new generation, one that you will be able to pour into and change.

You know what? They will think just like you! They are going to take the pattern that God has given you, and they are going to get excited about it because God Himself would have written it on their hearts! They are going to spread it to everyone they know. They will take it and re-teach it for themselves. It is going to spread like wildfire, and you will begin seeing the fruit of what you have labored for, for so long.

You will begin saying, "Hey, this pattern works! What the Lord taught me is real."

Driving the Vision Forward

This is the time when you will begin putting the pieces together. You see Moses didn't just stop there. He had the land that the Lord had given him mapped out, and he even divided it before they went into the Promised Land. He had everything set up, even the entire infrastructure.

Even though you have to leave the old generation behind, it doesn't mean it stops for you. The growing and the changing doesn't stop for you. No. There is still an unfolding ahead. In fact, there is a greater unfolding because now you have to know how to divide the land, who to put where, and who is going to take what part of the land.

You need to decide what belongs to who, and where, how and why they are going to go in. You need to decide what they are going to do when they get there, and how they will set things up. You have to set up an entire structure!

This is what the Lord did with us for our ministry centers and the fivefold training mechanism. We had to set up a structure. You see, it wasn't enough just to go out and teach people on the fivefold ministry. It is not enough for us just to stand here and preach and tell people what the fivefold ministry is. Sure, that is the anointed part and the ministry part, but then comes the practical side.

We have to put them together in an order and a structure. We added in workbooks so that people can take the lectures and apply them. We had to put in tests and exams to help put together a structure that is easy for people to follow.

Setting the Structure in Place

You can't just take a bunch of materials and throw it at them. You know, Moses could not walk into the Promised Land and say, "Here's the land guys. Help yourselves."

There would have been chaos! They wouldn't have known where to go first or what to do.

So, he said, "Well, this is the order. This is where you start. This is how the land should be divided, and this is who gets what piece of land."

He laid it all out. That is what the Moses apostle must do, and it is part of his mandate.

It is not enough to just stand and preach and give a whole lot of teaching. You have to put that teaching together in some kind of structure that can be re-used over and over again. It should be something that can remain as a foundation long after you have gone. It is not good enough just to see all these pieces that the Lord has given you and not see the final vision.

We could be standing here and preaching all these lectures and have them all listed in a big long list, and we could say, "Wow, look at all these lectures!"

You know, somebody coming in from the outside would not know where to start. It would look like chaos. It has been so rewarding to see us take those teachings and put them together in a structure. It has been great to put them in a pattern where they follow one after the other and start looking like something.

SEEING THE BIG PICTURE

It has been exciting to step back now and begin to see the whole picture and where all the pieces fit. It has been the most rewarding experience! For you, it is going to be the most rewarding experience towards the end of your mandate, to begin to see all the pieces that you have been working on all your life being put into this big picture.

Perhaps you had one little piece that never made any sense, and you said, "Lord, why did I have to learn this lesson? It makes absolutely no sense to me! It's in the middle of nowhere."

Suddenly, He will teach you a few more lessons, and that lesson will slot right in right where it should.

Often, when we do a teaching, I think, "Lord, this is a great teaching, but I don't know where it fits in. Where does it go?"

This is how it has been all along. You have gone through a training phase and learned something. Perhaps you have even preached it and put it together, but then it just sat gathering dust for a couple of years.

You think, "Did I waste my time with that? What did I experience that for? What did I face all of that for?"

Towards this stage of the journey, you are starting to see, "Oh, so that's why I had to face that! So that's why I had to deal with that."

You start putting it together, and it begins to look like something. In this very book, if you knew when they were taught, you would be surprised to discover that some of the chapters were taught 15 years apart!

There are times I will teach a message, and it will sit in the background for years before God allows me to publish it. At the moment, it feels like a piece of a puzzle that I do not have the picture of yet – to see where it fits. The more God leads me though, the more I see it come together.

Why these strange delays? It is because I believe God needed me to preach the message at that time to capture the anointing in that moment. It was the moment when the revelation was fresh. I had just lived it, and it captured all of that vision along with it.

Join a few of those together, and you discover that the Lord has been plotting your journey all along. To this day, when putting a book together, I stand in awe to discover that the missing piece for that book was a message that had been gathering dust for over 10 years. That was for this moment when it is even more relevant than at the time it was preached!

> *No season or experience has gone to waste.*

At the time, you might not always see where the pieces fit, but I promise you, they bring the power they were always intended to bring when they are slotted into place.

RESURRECTION TIME

This is your resurrection. The visions that you died to one at a time are now being resurrected together in one magnificent vision, and you are beginning to see it. It is right there in your grasp!

Another great part of your resurrection is that you will have with you your Joshuas and your Calebs. There will be those who will follow you all the way, through thick and thin.

They will say, "Moses, forget it. I want to see what happens at the end of this journey."

You see, they believe in you. They believe in your vision because it is their vision as well. They believe in what God has given you, and they will be those who will follow you right through to the end of the journey. They will want to know it all and will take the very life out of you, grabbing every bit of revelation.

They will be there on your heels, continually saying, "Give me more. Give me more! What is the Lord saying now? We believe in what God has put into you. What's next?"

In this ministry, there have been those who have been here since the very small beginnings who have followed through. They took the tests and trials, and the difficult things that came upon them, and they are still coming with us.

I am not sure if they are gluttons for punishment or just really zealous, but there they are. I turn around, and there they are. They are still hot on my heels. They are not letting go.

That is so rewarding! It is so rewarding to be able to share your successes with those who have been with you all along when you were nothing. With you, now suddenly, rising up to minister to all the masses that are there, it is great that they have known where you came from, and the small beginnings you had.

They are your real family! They will become part of you and what your ministry is. Even better, you will get to pour it out to them and give them everything.

Hand it Over

Then you will take all of it - the magnificent vision and everything it encompasses - and you will hand it over to Joshua. You will hand it over just when you can see it, just when it is right there!

You say, "It's right there in my grasp. I can see it. The pieces are coming together. The structure is starting to look like something real and solid. Man, what are they going to say about me when they see this? This is going to be big! It is going to go global! Everybody's going to be using this and applying it to their lives."

The Lord says, "That's wonderful Moses. You've done a tremendous job. I couldn't have done it without you. Now take everything, hand it over to Joshua, and go up the mountain one last time."

"Lord, I'm supposed to be leading the people through to the Promised Land!"

"Moses, you will! You see, your spirit is in those teachings. Your life is in that structure. Your very breath, and the essence of who and what you are, are in the people you have imparted to, Moses. You will be leading them to the Promised Land. You just won't be doing it in person!"

The Price

It is the greatest price that the Moses apostle has to pay, but he will live on forever. Who you are, and what you are, will remain in the hearts of God's people for as long as that foundation is solid. If you built the foundation correctly, and like Moses, did it exactly according to God's pattern and plan, it will stand.

We read how even in the days of David, the Tabernacle of Moses still stood that many years later! That foundation remained for thousands of years. It will not be shaken because it is built on the Word of God. It is built by His instruction, and you will live on through that foundation.

Isn't it like that with the Apostle Paul? I wonder if Paul knew when he was sitting in prison, writing those letters, that his very spirit in those words would be changing our lives two thousand years later? I wonder if he knew that he would still be alive this many years later, in our hearts and minds, and in the Word.

He never died. Though he did physically, his spirit remained. That is the greatest reward for the Moses apostle - knowing that in the heritage he leaves behind, he will remain alive forever. It is your greatest price, and your greatest reward, all bundled into one.

SUMMARY

To survive the wilderness of training, you need to begin by dying to self. You need to learn to lean on God. You need to pass the tests as fast as they come at you. The main purpose for your entire calling is to leave a heritage behind. This, Moses apostle, is what you are being called to do.

We are going to look next at how you will begin handing over that heritage to Joshua and all that it involves. Don't be discouraged, because I have a couple of surprises for you, and a couple of things you are not expecting to hear!

I just want you to commit yourself to the Lord again right now, and I want Him to encourage you. I want you to start seeing the full picture. I want you to start going back in your mind, even now, over all the little pieces of the puzzle that you have lived in your life over these many years.

There have been lots of little stages and fads that you have gone through. They seemed to die off, and then you went on another little fad and stage. You could never understand why you were going off in all those directions.

Right now, the Lord is bringing them together into one big picture, and He is slotting them like pieces of a puzzle to form a picture. I want you to begin seeking His face now to see the full picture of where everything lies.

"Thank you Holy Spirit for moving on your people. I pray for a spirit of revelation Lord. I ask you to go back through their entire lives and start pulling out all those pieces - every single one of them - and putting it together.

Let them see what their purpose is, what their calling is, why they are where they are, and where you are leading them. Let them know where their place is in this end-times move Lord. Raise them up. Send them forth, and give them the strength they need to stand in your cloud. In Jesus' name. Amen!"

CHAPTER 18

Birth, Maturation, Death and Resurrection

Chapter 18 – Birth, Maturation, Death and Resurrection

I invite you again in this chapter to go on a journey through the life of Moses. I have shared with you some of his preparation and training, and some of what you will face to be prepared for the Moses mandate - to carry out the plan that the Lord has for your life and for the body of Christ.

In this chapter, I will share a lot of pictures and images with you, and I want you to see these pictures as I take you along. I want you to see the life of Moses. I want you to feel and hear and smell and taste his life, because, this is the life you will live as a Moses apostle.

Make it Real

I am going to begin now by sharing a passage out of Deuteronomy 34:1. As you read this passage, I want you to see the pictures in this passage. I want you to feel as Moses felt, and imagine what he must have gone through.

So, as I do this, I want you to receive revelation for yourself. I don't want you to just read this chapter and fill your head with knowledge. I want you to receive your own conviction, your own revelation, and your own understanding.

I want you to live your own journey that is special to you, because it is not enough simply to read these chapters. It is not enough just to understand them. It is not even enough to apply the projects in them. They must become your own conviction. They must become part of who and what you are. You must live them, and you must know them from experience, not just from understanding.

Deuteronomy 34:1 *Then Moses went up from the plains of Moab to Mount Nebo, to the top of Pisgah, which is across from Jericho. And the Lord showed him all the land of Gilead as far as Dan,*

2 all Naphtali and the land of Ephraim and Manasseh, all the land of Judah as far as the Western Sea,[a]

3 the South, and the plain of the Valley of Jericho, the city of palm trees, as far as Zoar.

4 Then the Lord said to him, "This is the land of which I swore to give Abraham, Isaac, and Jacob, saying, 'I will give it to your descendants.' I have caused you to see it with your eyes, but you shall not cross over there."

5 So Moses the servant of the Lord died there in the land of Moab, according to the word of the Lord.

6 And He buried him in a valley in the land of Moab, opposite Beth Peor; but no one knows his grave to this day.

7 Moses was one hundred and twenty years old when he died. His eyes were not dim nor his natural vigor diminished.

8 And the children of Israel wept for Moses in the plains of Moab thirty days. So the days of weeping and mourning for Moses ended.

9 Now Joshua the son of Nun was full of the spirit of wisdom, for Moses had laid his hands on him; so the children of Israel heeded him, and did as the Lord had commanded Moses.

10 But since then there has not arisen in Israel a prophet like Moses, whom the Lord knew face to face,

11 in all the signs and wonders which the Lord sent him to do in the land of Egypt, before Pharaoh, before all his servants, and in all his land,

12 and by all that mighty power and all the great terror which Moses performed in the sight of all Israel.

There was never a prophet, and there was never a man who showed the might and the glory of God as Moses did. That is your reward, apostle of God - that there was never a prophet such as Moses who moved in the power and in the glory of God.

Yet, with the reward came the greatest sacrifice that Moses would ever have to face! That sacrifice was that he would never see the land with his eyes. He would know the land with his understanding, but he would never lead the children of Israel in to possess that land.

A Continual Process

As I take you through the life of the training of Moses, I want you to see all four stages that you will pass through - the birth, the maturation, the death, and the resurrection of your vision.

This is what you will experience and live as a Moses apostle, because it is a process that you will live again and again. Just when you thought, "Lord, this is the final death I have to face," you will be called to another death.

It depends on you on how you want to go, how far you want to resurrect. You see, you can stop along this road right now.

You can stop right here and say, "I've had enough of the death, thank you very much. I've had enough of the persecution. I have had enough of the sacrifice," and you could remain where you are.

Or, you could go for the greater prize, that it would be said of you, as it was said of Moses, "There was no greater prophet in the land of Israel who knew the power and the glory of God."

It comes with a great price, apostle. It comes with a chance that the men to come may not know your name. Moses had to hand over to Joshua with the knowledge that when Joshua took over, the people could forget about him. It was possible that Joshua may not even carry things out as he had laid out.

That was the sacrifice that he had to make. If Moses had not been prepared to pay that price, Israel would not have seen the resurrection that was to come.

THE BIRTH — THE BURNING BUSH

We begin with the birth, where your mandate begins. We have shared the process of having to face the wilderness, climbing the mountain, and having an experience with the Lord. It is the burning bush experience where you receive your mandate from the Lord.

It was here that Moses received his mandate and was sent to Egypt to confront Pharaoh. There was the battle and the signs and wonders, and it was magnificent.

Moses didn't start off slowly. He got right in where the action was. This baby was born screaming. It was not a long travail for Moses. Yes, his preparation was long. He spent forty years in preparation, but when the training began, it began with a bang!

He didn't ease into his mandate. He was not like David who kind of built up over the years. No, Moses was in his boots and all right from the very beginning.

He received the Word from the Lord and was sent directly to Egypt. He confronted Pharaoh and then came the signs, and persecutions in Egypt with all the plagues. There was conflict and fighting, and he argued with Pharaoh.

He was always in a position of needing to convince the people of Israel, and the elders, of what God promised. Then, the people of Israel stood against him, because Pharaoh was coming down hard on them. He had to stand his ground.

It was a battle and a fight. It was a process of winning and losing – a constant struggle! It was no small struggle either. It was at a huge magnitude.

This wasn't a little inner struggle that he battled with on the top of the mountain. No, this was something on a large scale. He was confronting the King of Egypt and all his hordes. It was right out there. It wasn't a hidden little struggle where nobody could notice. Moses was thrust there, into the thick of it, where everybody could see him face it.

Immediate Visibility

Moses had it tough. He couldn't afford to fail, even in his training, because he was right out there in the public eye where everybody could see him. He had to contend with the system right at the top where everybody could notice. Some of them liked it, and some of them didn't.

The elders thought it was a great idea, but the children of Israel didn't think it was too much fun when Pharaoh started putting the pressure on them. Was Moses going to make it, or was he going to fail?

I don't think he had much of a choice. He had already gotten in there and had already burned his bridges. There was nowhere to go but forward. He pushed forward, and signs and wonders followed.

It was glorious and magnificent! Then came the final plague, and the firstborn of all Egypt was killed. The angel of the Lord came down and swept over the whole of Egypt, and the children of Israel were saved. They were redeemed and set free!

Signs and Wonders

There was glory after glory, signs and wonders. From the day that vision was birthed, the baby screamed, and its voice was heard throughout the nations.

That is your mandate, Moses apostle. Your vision will be birthed. Your ministry will be birthed. The day that it is birthed, the cry of that vision will go out through all the nations. There will be many who will hear the voice of that child, and they will look up to see where it is coming from.

This is no time to fail, no time to miss it. There is a job to be done. There is a work to be completed, and you will follow through to the end because you have no choice now.

You know when a baby is being born, you can't say, "Hang on a minute, I'll just put it back. I'm not ready for it yet!"

It doesn't work that way. This baby has been born, and it is screaming loudly. You have to follow this job through to the end.

TRAINING ON THE RUN

So, all this preparation that you have faced suddenly comes into play, as well as all that death, having to deal with the Pharaoh within you, and having to confront the fear of Pharaoh.

Suddenly, you realize you are coping with things in ways you never could before. You are handling it in a better way than you handled it before. You are being trained on the run. You are being molded into His image. You are going up the mountain, and one after the other, things are happening.

Moses landed with his feet running. Moses apostle, when the call comes, and the mandate is given to you, you will land with your feet running. You will not ease into it.

It will come on you suddenly like a woman in travail as the Scriptures say. It will come on you suddenly, and the travail will be fast. The birth will be fast, and the growth of the child will be speedy. The birth is glorious and magnificent.

So began a journey after the birth of this child, and Moses led the children of Israel out of Egypt. Now they were faced with the Red Sea. Here was another obstacle. What happened? The Lord parted the Red Sea.

It was another wonderful sign, and millions were there to watch the magnificent birth of this baby. They were there to see it start growing, and it was incredible! The mandate was showing itself. The ministry was being proven with signs and wonders following.

Moses didn't have time to sit around anymore. He was busy. He had a job to do. He didn't have time to sit in the backside of the desert. There was action needed. What had taken place before was gone. He didn't even think about those sheep anymore! He also didn't even think about his father-in-law anymore. He was too busy doing.

YOUR PAST REMAINS BEHIND

Moses apostle, as you start now with the mandate that the Lord has given you, all those things of the past - everything you achieved and everything the Lord used to make you what you are now - it will all become a faint distant memory.

It will be a part of your past and will be no more. Your life will be before and after the call, because you will be two different people. There will be two different lives, like day and night.

The birth of the baby will come suddenly and loudly upon you, and it will be magnificent! It will be just what you need to start leading the children of Israel and the people of God in the right direction. Just like a rocket needs all the fuel and power under it to launch it through to the stars, so will you need this power to launch you.

Once you are there, it is a little easier. Then, you don't need much power because you don't have gravity any longer. To launch it would be like a rocket bursting into outer space. It takes a tremendous amount of power and energy to get it going. The power and glory will come, and it will launch you as your ministry is birthed for all the world to see.

Then, it is sustained. It seems as if there is one miracle after the next. The children of Israel had barely crossed the Red Sea, and the Lord was giving them water out of the rock. He was giving them manna on the floor to gather and eat. The Lord gave them quail for meat. There was one thing after the next.

Moses just could not fail. There was nothing that he could do wrong. The baby begins to live and grow and be nourished, and it is looking chubby. It is looking healthy and doing well. Hope is beginning to spring in your heart. You are starting to see this as a possibility.

You are thinking, "Hey, I can do this thing! I can accomplish this task that the Lord has given me to do. I know I can make it."

So, we see this journey progressing from the wilderness and the top of the mountain to Egypt, through the Red Sea. There was the manna and water out of the rock, the quail, the miracles, one after the other, and the baby was starting to grow.

The Lord was not finished with Moses just yet. It wasn't enough for the baby just to be born. It wasn't enough for it to just get chubby. He had to feed this ministry. He had to grow it up and mature it. He needed to lay a foundation.

THE MATURATION: COMMANDMENTS AND PRECEPTS

I shared on how Moses revisited the mountain, time and time again, and how the Lord started giving him the Law. He started laying a foundation and getting a picture now of what he was really called to do.

You see, Moses had this idea, "All I'm really called to do is to go and get the children of Israel out of Egypt and take them to the Promised Land. I mean, that seems easy enough!"

When you are first called, that is what you think. The Lord has given you a vision or picture, but unbeknown to you, it is a limited vision. It is just the first step.

That really isn't the ultimate goal that the Lord has for you. He has a bigger vision in mind, and He had a bigger vision in mind for Moses. He didn't just intend for him to take the children of Israel to the Promised Land. The real mandate that God had for Moses was to lay a new foundation for the generations to come.

Moses was simply a catalyst in getting the children of Israel out of Egypt. His actual mandate was to lay a foundation for the generations to come. I have shared on this already. He needed to set up a structure that they could use, generation after generation, to serve the Lord.

You Bring the Mandate to Maturation

That is your real mandate, apostle of God. The glory is magnificent and the anointing is wonderful, but that is not the main thrust of your ministry. The main thrust of your ministry is to lay a foundation. Don't ever forget that! Don't get so caught up in the signs and wonders, the glory and the external anointing, that you forget your real purpose.

This is the main reason that the Lord has had to train His apostles in secret. It is because He has given much of His power and glory to part the Sea and call forth the manna and water from the rock. They became so caught up in the glory and the signs and wonders that they did not bring the mandate to maturity.

It is so much fun to part the Red Sea! It is glorious to scoop up the manna, and wonderful to jump in the river. It's not so glorious though to climb the mountain without any food and water, day after day, to receive a bunch of writing on a piece of stone!

It's not so glorious to be separated unto God, where nobody can see you all alone on top of the mountain, to receive that pattern that you will not even see implemented in your lifetime! What is so glorious about that?

If you are not prepared to pay that price, then resign right now because it is not just about the glory. It's about completing the mandate the Lord gave you.

Had Apostle Paul not completed his mandate, we would not have the New Testament today. Do you think he realized, when he was sitting in a prison writing to people he didn't even know, that his words would be read two thousand years later?

You see, Paul had flowed in signs and the wonders. He knew all about it. They used to take cloths from his body and lay them on the sick, and they were healed. He started churches and had huge campaigns.

He knew the glory. He knew the warfare and the anointing. He knew what it was like to be that rocket being shot into the heavens. Where was the glory when he was sitting in prison writing his letters to his churches?

FUTURE GENERATIONS

Let me tell you something, apostle. Had he not sat and written those letters, we would not have known about the glory. Who would have heard of Paul? Who would have cared? What would his anointing have done for the church of God today? It would have done nothing!

> *The anointing is magnificent, and the glory is wonderful. But, until a structure is set in place, all of that will fade.*

It will go away, because the glory of God can only be contained in His Word. Had His Word not been put down for us, we would not have known of that glory.

You can move in all the signs and wonders that you like. But, unless you take the glory that the Lord has given you and put it into a structure for the generations to come, they will never know it. Your life will be a waste.

You will come and go, and be like the flower and the grass which shines and grows beautifully today, but tomorrow, it is like the dust.

It is great now, but you know what? I am not in this so that I can shine today and fade tomorrow. When they bury me, the mandate that God has given me must continue on from generation to generation. Otherwise, all the years that He has spent training me have been a waste of time.

What use is it to glow and shine today, for today's generation that doesn't go on tomorrow? Then, the Lord has to take another vessel to train them up their entire lives for the same thing, and then, He has to start from scratch again.

Imagine if Paul hadn't written his letters. The Lord would have had to raise up another apostle, so that he would write it down and so that we would have something.

It is not enough to only shine today. You must take the glory, the signs and wonders, and all these things that God has given to you, and begin piecing it together into a structure. That is your mandate.

Your mandate is not to have revival meetings or to call down the glory. That is just an additional benefit. Your mandate is to lay a foundation and to put a structure together for the generations to come.

Do not get so caught up in the glory cloud that you forget to descend the mountain to bring the cloud down to the people, because that is what you are called to do.

If you are not prepared to pay that price, and if you are getting so carried away in the glory that you cannot bring it down to the people, then you are a waste of time. God will pass you by and raise up another in your stead.

God's Way or No Way

Some wonder why I am so hard on the apostles - and I am. If somebody comes to me and says, "I'm called to the apostolic ministry," I am very hard, and I do test.

Why do I test them? I test them because being an apostle is not a game. Being an apostle is not like playing chess to see who wins or loses. It is not something you go by the seat of your pants and say, "Oh well, I've got nothing else to do this year. I will be an apostle."

These are the lives of God's people that you have in your hands - not just the generation of today but the generation of tomorrow.

This is God's plan you're messing with here, and you don't make adjustments when you feel like it.

You don't say, "Well, thank you Lord for the pattern for the tent of meeting, but you know what? I'm going to leave out the cherubim. I didn't like the cherubim on the Tabernacle.

"Did you like them? I just didn't like the idea of having them on, and quite honestly, I don't feel like it. I want to go and part the Red Sea. You know what, Lord? We'll just leave the cherubim off."

It doesn't work that way. It is all or nothing! You are either going to complete the entire pattern, or you're not going to do it at all. You're going to build the tent, and the Tabernacle with its cherubim and all the things that go with it, or it is nothing.

You are either following this thing through to the letter the way God says, the way He wants it and in His timetable, or you're not doing it at all.

> **There is no space for selfish motivation. There is no time to go on a revival kick.**

There is a job to be done, and there is a short space in which to do it. Moses apostle, until you have finished your job, Joshua cannot come and complete it. There is no time to mess around.

How many more generations must we wait for? For how many more generations must the church of God lie in the scum and slum of this earth? How many more generations must see our youth being distracted by the ways of the world? For how many more generations must we watch our society deteriorate year after year?

How many more generations? It depends on you, because, until you have finished laying the structure, the next ones cannot come to implement it. They must implement the structure you have set up. Only then will we begin seeing the church of God rising up into the full glory that she has been called to be.

Do you see how important your role is? There is no place for mistakes. There's no place for bad attitudes. There's no place for self-exaltation or a need for recognition. There's no place for getting carried away in the signs. You need to commit to the job at hand. You need to put your hand to the work God has given you, and that is to lay the structure.

Pour Into Your Sons

As you are laying the structure, this is when the Lord will give you your Joshua.

The Lord is going to bring you those who will be your sons. It is up to you to take everything that God has put into you, and pour it into them. Your mandate and the future of the Church depends on what you pour into your spiritual sons and daughters.

Are you prepared to take that pattern, to take everything you have, and give it away? That is what God requires you to do. If you want to hog it and not pass it on, then it will die with you.

We have seen many great revivalists come and go. They died, and nobody ever heard about them. If others had not risen up and written books about them, we wouldn't have even known they existed. The only people who knew they existed were the ones whose lives they changed.

Nobody else knew. They died, and they left no heritage whatsoever. They took the anointing and all the revelation that God had given them - all the great revivalists that moved in tremendous power and glory - and they died with it.

We look at Kathryn Kuhlman. We look at Maria Woodworth-Etter and Aimee Semple-McPherson. We look at all of these people. They were magnificent! They shone so brightly in their day. When they died, the revival died with them because they didn't pass it on to another. They didn't take a spiritual son or daughter and give of their very essence to them and pour out everything that God had given them.

This cannot happen with the revival that is to come. If you think you have seen revival, you haven't seen anything yet! What has been happening in the body of Christ just before the twentieth century is such a small tidbit of what is about to take place after the twentieth century. That is going to blow the world!

It is going to blow its mind. You haven't seen a thing yet! The end-times apostles will bring a move to the Church To this world, that is going to shatter nations! It starts with you, Moses apostle. It starts with the structure you are going to put down.

Pass it Down

The Lord is raising up those who have the commitment to pass down to others what He has put into them. The Lord does not have time to raise another from the bottom all the way up again, so that He can try and build up another generation.

> *The ones who are to come after you must start off where you ended. They must not have to go and start all the way at the beginning again.*

I look at my own children, and I look at my life and my upbringing. By the time I was in my teens, I was functioning in the church. While my father was called at twenty, I was called at thirteen. Where he started preaching at twenty-two, I gave my first message when I was fourteen.

I was immediately thrust into the call of God because of everything that was imparted to me. I look at how he had to go through all those struggles, and by my early twenties, I was standing up and preaching and standing fully in Prophetic Office, where it took him years to achieve it.

Then, I look at my children, my eldest, who at the age of six already functioned in prophetic ministry. At 21, married and the principle of our prophetic school, being used as a prophet in office to minister internationally side by side with her husband.

Do you know why that is possible? It is possible because my father took everything he had and gave it to me, and I stepped into his finished work and passed it on. I ran with it and imparted it to my natural and spiritual children. Now they, too, can rise up and run the race!

Just imagine what the next generation will be like. Why can't a born again believer raise the dead? That can only take place if we impart everything we have to those the Lord brings us.

Can you see the end goal? Can you see the part you have to play? We all fit into this grand plan. Find out where you fit and complete your task to the best of your ability, and you will see things happen in the earth even today that will blow your mind.

Allow somebody else to step into your finished work, and watch them rise up beyond you - at a younger age, with greater zeal, and a more powerful anointing.

Yet, with that more powerful anointing, and with that zeal and charisma, they will just be pouring out what you have given them, and what the Lord has given you.

They will have your spirit, and everything that God has given you. You will live your life through them, and you will never die. Though your body may pass away, your mandate will remain because of what God put into you, and because of what you put into others.

IMPLEMENT THE PATTERN

You need to put the final structure into place. Moses came along, and he didn't just receive the pattern. He implemented it.

He said, "Joshua, this is how it works."

He set up the Tabernacle, built it just as the Lord had shown him to build it, and he set it in place. Just like David set everything up for Solomon, going and getting all the materials he needed to build the temple, so Moses also did with Joshua.

He didn't just get the Law. He didn't just get the pattern. He put everything into place for Joshua. He took a whole map of the land, and he said, "Okay, this is how it should be split up," and he divided the land ahead of time.

He set up the Tabernacle. He set up the ordinances and the laws for worship, the laws for sacrifice, for public holidays - the laws for everything! He set everything in place, and he began to implement it.

He began teaching and instructing the people on how to apply the laws and what they needed to do in certain cases. He started putting it into practice. He taught it to them until it was a part of them. He set up the whole infrastructure for Joshua just to step in and take over.

TRIAL AND ERROR

It is not enough just to know in your head what needs to be done. You need to try this thing out. You need to have some kind of maiden voyage or practice session. You need to practically apply what the Lord has given you to see if it works, just like I taught in the teaching, *Driving Your Vision Forward.*

I remember when we first started the training schools and how it seemed like the Lord was swapping us here, there, and everywhere, doing so many different things. However, in hindsight, I see how He was forcing us to implement the vision that He had given us.

When we had implemented a portion of the vision, He would say, "Okay, time to try out something else."

Man, did we fail! We succeeded, but we also failed. We learned and bumped our heads a few times. We learned the hard way what to do, and what not to do, what worked and what didn't work.

Now, as you take all of this knowledge and training that you faced, when your Joshua comes along you say,

"Here you go. This is what works and what doesn't work. This is where you need to go and how you need to divide the land.

This is how you build up the Tabernacle and put it together. This is how you disassemble it and how you reassemble it. Don't do it in the rain. Wait for a sunny day."

You give him a whole picture.

As we look at our experiences and the trials and errors we learned from them, we are now qualified to say to others, "This is how you start a ministry. This is what you don't do. This is how you launch a church. This is how you set up a training center. This is how you train a prophet. Don't do this. Do that. This is how you train an apostle. This is how you train a pastor. This is what works. This is what doesn't work."

You give them the full vision, and you say, "Go and do it!" and they step into your finished work. They apply everything you have given them, and they can look magnificent.

People say, "Wow, you're something else! You just step in there and know what to do."

Well of course they do! They listened to you. They received everything you gave them. That is a joy, to see your spiritual sons and daughters come, take everything you have taught them, go apply it, and be a success.

The Lord will lead you to step in and start a new work, to start and implement the pattern that He has given you. You are going to piece it all together. You will make it look incredible! You will go through the trials and errors. You will have to handle the Israelites moaning at you all the time, and having to fall on your face before the Lord to get the answers.

The Treasures We Have to Impart

You know, if you read Joshua, you don't see him making as many mistakes as Moses did, because he learned from Moses' mistakes.

He learned from Moses' trials and errors and entered into his finished work.

You are going to head out there, and you are going to try it. You will fail, and you will succeed. You are going to move in the signs and wonders, and you are going to gain experience, knowledge, and wisdom.

As you gain these things, the Lord will bring you your Joshua. He is going to stand by your side, and you will pour everything into him until he starts acting and thinking just like you. The Law and pattern that God has given you will become his. Suddenly, your Joshua doesn't know what is his mandate and what is your mandate anymore because you seem so blended.

He must become a replica of you, but without all your mistakes, errors, and weaknesses.

That is exactly what he will become, because he will have learned from your mistakes. There will come a time where he rises up as your spiritual son, until people say, "Wow, I can see you are related!" They will be able to identify you in him.

CHAPTER 19

HANDING OVER TO JOSHUA

Chapter 19 – Handing Over to Joshua

Death: Returned to the Wilderness

Then comes the beginning of a very painful process. Just as the vision was birthed, the glory came and the rocket shot up into the stars, then comes death. Everything was awesome. It was gaining momentum, and then it began to die.

The children of Israel disobeyed the Lord. Moses sent in the spies, thinking, "This is it! I'm right here. I'm at the Promised Land. We'll send in the spies. They will come back, and we can go in and conquer the land.

"Milk and honey, here we come! I know it. It is within my grasp. I've tried this pattern. I've implemented it, and it is working. I've got my Joshua by my side. He's a magnificent general! He fights the armies while I sit and put down the pattern. We're a magnificent team."

You think, "This is great! The ministry is flourishing. People know us from all over the world now. It's really something else. The Lord has done such a work. The end is within sight."

However, the people balked, and the Lord said, "That's it! You're wandering in the desert for forty years."

Moses said, "Oh Lord, another forty years! It was right there."

The Lord said, "It's time to die. You've got to let it go."

It got worse. Moses became so angry with the people when they cried out for water that, instead of speaking to the rock as God had commanded him, he struck the rock and directly disobeyed the Lord.

The Lord said to him, "That's it, Moses! You're not even going into the Promised Land! Never mind you are not leading the people in there, you're not even going to step into the Promised Land. It is over!"

"Lord, what was it for? What was the power for? What was the glory for? What was the anointing for? Not to ever see it come to pass?"

CONFUSION AND STRUGGLES

Sometimes, you feel that way. You pour into people, and you work hard. You pour and strive and give, and you never seem to see the fruit of it.

You say, "I don't get it. I don't see the point in standing up here and preaching and giving, and nobody gets it. They stand up and spout off the biggest load of garbage that tells me they didn't hear a word I said! They haven't changed. They are still in their old ways. Lord, I don't see the point in this?"

I don't know how many times I personally have had this struggle with the Lord.

I say, "Lord, it's not fair. Do you know how much I've poured into them? Do you know how much I strive with these people?"

The Lord said, "You think you've got it bad? You are going to die. I'm left with them!"

You know, the strange thing is that those people you were ready to just give up on will surprise you one day. They will stand up behind the pulpit and talk just like you! Then, you will know that the foundation that you laid is bearing much fruit.

Sometimes, you might not see that fruit, Moses, but the fruit is there. If the foundation is Jesus Christ, it will remain sturdy from generation to generation. You have no fear. It will remain. Your job is to lay that foundation and to set up the structure for the generations to come.

From the time Moses disobeyed God and struck the rock, there were no more miracles from the hand of Moses. There was a steady decline – a complete death. It was as if everything was removed from Moses. His anointing, his prophetic insight, his experiences with the Lord - everything seemed to be taken away.

So, you start out great. There are the signs and the wonders. You set up the ministry. You set up the structure. You have tried it and tested it, and then it seems like everything starts to die. The anointing ebbs. The revival starts to slow down. The people start wandering off and doing their own thing, and nobody wants to listen to you anymore.

You say, "What is going on Lord? You called me to this task. You told me that this is the direction I must go in. You said I must build this work, and now it's dying! I don't understand why it must die."

Time to Hand Over

The Lord is saying, "Upon the cross, Moses. It's time to die. It's time to let it go and to hand over to Joshua. Your time here is done. It's over!"

That is the very first sign that time is approaching to hand over to Joshua. Joshua has risen up and is thinking just like you. He is standing by your side. He has become a leader in his own right now. Then suddenly, the anointing starts to leave you.

No, you haven't missed it. No, you have not failed God. No, you didn't miss it with the pattern that He has given you. It is just time to hand over. It is time to move on and to let the next generation take over from you.

> *That is your first sign. The anointing ebbs.*

You have started a work, and everything has been glorious. Now suddenly, things have started slowing down, and you are thinking, "What is going on?"

If this is happening, it is time to hand over to Joshua and move on. It is time to let it go. It is not a pleasant experience. Then, it gets worse!

You say, "What?! Worse? What can be worse than losing the glory? What can be worse than losing the signs and the wonders and the miracles? What can be worse than the people suddenly wanting to rebel against me and me losing the respect that is due to me? What can be worse than having to say goodbye to my whole vision that I have been striving towards all these years?"

GOD BYPASSES YOU

What is worse is that God passes over you and speaks to Joshua. It says in Deuteronomy 31:14:

> *Then the Lord said to Moses, "Behold, the days approach when you must die; call Joshua, and present yourselves in the tabernacle of meeting, that I may inaugurate him."*
>
> *So Moses and Joshua went and presented themselves in the tabernacle of meeting.*

For the first time, God bypassed Moses and gave Joshua the charge. He said, "Joshua, this is what I want you to do. I want you to take the children of Israel to the next level."

It was devastating! Moses had received the direction for the people of Israel before now. He was the one who received the revelation and who spoke to God face-to-face. He was the one where the Lord said, "Okay, it's time to pack up and move to the next place."

He was the one who the Lord told to send in the spies, and who received all the direction and got the revelation for the ministry. He received the next phase that they needed to go through. He was the one who opened and closed doors, who turned the key and locked it.

The final death knell came when the Lord gave the next direction to Joshua. When God begins passing you by and starts giving the revelation to your Joshua, realize it is your call to death. Don't get defensive and try to grab control, and squash your Joshua into the ground.

Realize that it is time to die, and that your time there is over. It is finished! It is time to die Moses, to let the vision go. It is time for Joshua to take your place.

IT IS MEANT TO HAPPEN

Why are you so worried, and why are you so distraught about it? Is that not what you are meant to do? Is it not the whole purpose of your mandate – to pass it down to another? What are you so devastated about? You have succeeded! That is what you were meant to do - to do yourself out of a job.

You say, "It has become so comfortable. It has become cushy here in this job. It is nice. I've started to calm down. Things have become easier. I'm not having to confront Pharaoh anymore. There are miracles of manna and quails every day.

"You know what? I've become cozy here. We've set up this nice ministry. The finances are pouring in. People know who I am. I'm famous and well known! It's wonderful. Why would I want to give all this up?"

It is because you are a Moses. You're supposed to give it all up and start all over again. That is what you are called to do, otherwise, you wouldn't be a Moses. That is your job. Congratulate yourself. You did your job well.

When God starts passing you over and raising your Joshua up in your stead, instead of being discouraged, you can rejoice and say, "I have succeeded in the mandate that God has given me! I can now go, knowing that this will come to pass."

It says this in Deuteronomy 31:23. It is the Lord speaking:

> *Then He inaugurated Joshua the son of Nun, and said, "Be strong and of good courage; for you shall bring the children of Israel into the land of which I swore to them, and I will be with you."*

The Lord passed over Moses and gave it to Joshua and said, "Okay Joshua, you are taking the people of Israel to the next level."

GIVEN TO ANOTHER

God handed Israel over to Joshua, not Moses. God will take your ministry and vision, and He will give it to another. He will give it to your Joshua, whether you like it or not. You can fight it, and you can struggle. You can scream and jump up and down, but it doesn't help. God has given it to another. Step back gracefully, and know it is time to die.

Suddenly, now Joshua heard from God for himself. Up until this point, your Joshua has needed you to hear from the Lord. Now, there comes a time when you have trained and mentored him so well that he can hear from God for himself.

He does not need you there. Hey, he is going to miss you. He will miss you like mad, but he doesn't need you anymore - not to that extent. You can now step back, allowing your spiritual son to rise up into adulthood.

Be proud of what you put into him! Be proud, knowing that he is going to go out there, and act just like you. He is going to go and do everything you told him to. Be proud and rejoice. This is a day for celebration, not a day for mourning, because something magnificent is going to happen as you die and let it go. Look at Joshua 1:1-3. It says:

> *After the death of Moses, the servant of the Lord, it came to pass that the Lord spoke to Joshua the son of Nun, Moses' assistant, saying:*
>
> *2 "Moses My servant is dead. Now therefore, arise, go over this Jordan, you and all this people, to the land which I am giving to them—the children of Israel.*
>
> *3 Every place that the sole of your foot will tread upon I have given you, as I said to Moses.*

Resurrection: Taking the Promised Land

Then comes the resurrection, and you may not be there to see it because you will have had to die, step back, and hand that vision over to Joshua. You will stand from afar, Moses, and you will watch that resurrection come forth in glory and power, just as God told you it would happen.

Do you know what? It gets better! That is just the crossing of the Jordan. Your death is just a door. As you step into that death, you will release that vision and ministry that God has caused you to lay the foundation for. Then, that Joshua of yours will take that vision to the next level.

They will cross that Jordan, and they will walk in the Law that God has given you, and they will use the structure that God has given you. It gets better however. In Joshua 22:4:

> *And now the Lord your God has given rest to your brethren, as He promised them; now therefore, return and go to your tents and to the land of your possession, which Moses the servant of the Lord gave you on the other side of the Jordan.*

Now comes the time when they have the whole of the Promised Land. They didn't just cross over into the Promised Land. You didn't just get to see them cross over that Jordan. You got to see them take the whole Promised Land!

They didn't just take the whole land, but they had a time of rest and a time to be conquerors. Why? It is because of what you laid out and the structure that you set up. The church of God will benefit, and they will enter into the fullness of the Promised Land, and be resurrected beyond anything you would have imagined.

Yes, Moses, the glory is going to come, but you need to know when to let go. As you let go and allow your Joshua to take over, it will release the Lord to take it to the next level.

This is because, had you not completed the mandate, Joshua could not come and accomplish what he did accomplish.

A Continual Cycle

You will share in the victories of Joshua, and you will share in the glory to come, time and time again. Moses, it is not over because there will be another birth, and there will be another death. There will be another resurrection for as long as you live.

The Lord will send you again and again to get into a place, to birth a ministry, to set up its structure and set it in place. You will raise up a Joshua and lay your hands on him and impart everything you have. Then you will hand it over, step back, and watch it pass from resurrection to glory. Then, Moses, you will step into another place.

You are not going to have a very boring life. You will not settle in one place. Your job is to go in, lay the foundation, get the structure set up, hand over to Joshua, and move on.

Don't get cozy. I know that the Moses apostle is primarily analytical, and all of us know that analyticals like to be comfortable. They like the cozy little arrangement where everything is set in place. Moses strived so hard to get structured and organized that, by the time he finally arrived there, he thought, "Thank the Lord I can take a break!"

Just when he got to that point, the Lord said, "Okay, time to move on again."

More chaos! He said, "Oh Lord, can't I get comfortable for just one minute?"

No, sorry, you can't stay comfortable, because just as you start getting that cozy feeling that says, "You know what? I like it here! This is good stuff," the Lord says, "No Moses, it's time to move again."

Don't get comfortable. Do not be complacent and satisfied for just one vision. I don't want just one vision. I want them all! I don't want just one nation. I want them all! I don't want one State of America. I want them all!

Well, how many years do you have? You had better get moving. There is a job to be done. For the rest of your life, you will go from birth to maturity, to death, to resurrection, and round and round again, for as long as you desire and want to.

Like I said at the beginning, you can stop this process any time you like, but then you will never know what the resurrection looks like. You will also never get to see what it is like for that vision to enter into glory.

If you really are a Moses apostle, there is no way you would want to give that up, because God has put that passion in you. That is what makes you unique, and it is what gives you the glory to go on and on.

Moses apostle, a tremendous task is ahead of you! I know that with the power and glory of God, you will not only accomplish that task, but you will take the church of God from glory to glory.

About the Author

Born in Bulawayo, Zimbabwe and raised in South Africa, Colette had a zeal to serve the Lord from a young age. Coming from a long line of Christian leaders and having grown up as a pastor's kid, she is no stranger to the realities of ministry. Despite having to endure many hardships such as her parent's divorce, rejection, and poverty, she continues to follow after the Lord passionately.

Overcoming these obstacles early in her life has built a foundation of compassion and desire to help others gain victory in their lives.

Since then, the Lord has led Colette, with her husband, Craig Toach, to establish *Apostolic Movement International,* a ministry to train and minister to Christian leaders all over the world, where they share all the wisdom that the Lord has given them through each and every time they chose to walk through the refining fire in their personal lives, as well as in ministry.

In addition, Colette is a fantastic cook, an amazing mom to not only her 4 natural children, but to her numerous spiritual children all over the world. Colette is also a renowned author, mentor, trainer and a woman that has great taste in shoes! The scripture to "be all things to all men" definitely applies here, and the Lord keeps adding to that list of things each and every day.

How does she do it all? Experience through every book and teaching the life of an apostle firsthand, and get the insight into how the call of God can make every aspect of your life an incredible adventure.

Read more at www.colette-toach.com

Connect with Colette Toach on Facebook!
www.facebook.com/ColetteToach

Recommendations by the Author

Note: All reference of AMI refers to Apostolic Movement International.

If you enjoyed this book, we know you will also love the following books.

The Apostolic Mandate

Book 1 of the Apostolic Field Guide Series

By Colette Toach

As one called to be an apostle, there is a fire in your bones that cannot be contained. The Lord Jesus himself has given you a mandate, and a commission, that seeks its rightful place in the earth.

However, there is a problem. The task at hand can seem overwhelming and the implementation too great, if the foundation is not laid correctly.

Follow Colette Toach in this book as she takes you down this exciting and empowering road to finding your true mandate from God.

The Apostolic Handbook

By Colette Toach

This book has the potential to not only confirm your calling, but launch you headfirst into the training that will take you to apostolic office.

If you have the suspicion or the strong conviction that you have been called to be an apostle, then you are on for the adventure of a lifetime. In fact, you hold in your hands a treasure map that gives you clear directions.

This book will not only tell you everything you need to know about this ministry office, but it will also TAKE YOU THERE!

DRIVING YOUR VISION FORWARD (MP3)

By Colette Toach

When Moses went into the wilderness, it was not for forever, but for a season where he had to grow and mature and where he had to become the vessel that God needed to set His people free. Once Moses was ready, God called him out of the desert.

If you desire to lead God's people out of Egypt, then it is time you receive your "burning bush" experience, and see just where exactly God wants you to lead them.

HOW TO GET PEOPLE TO FOLLOW YOU

By Colette Toach

"You have the potential for something magnificent, but until you can get your boat into the water and unfurl those sails... you are not going anywhere. " - Colette Toach

Colette pours out leadership secrets straight from the Throne Room that will make you the kind of leader others want to follow. No more hitting your head on the wall. No more being the only one excited about your vision.

Sharing from her own failures and triumphs, Colette hands you the keys to your success as a leader.

MENTORSHIP 101

By Colette Toach

Mentorship! What picture comes into your mind? It is a very hot topic in the Church today, but clear teaching is lacking. In this series, you will not only find out what the role and purpose of a mentor is, but you will see the heart that is required!

For indeed mentorship is not just about imparting knowledge, but about being a vessel for the Holy Spirit. So that He can flow through you to mold and shape your disciple. Mentorship costs a price, for both the mentor and disciple, but it is what will bring fruit that truly remains.

God is raising up His Mighty Warrior, and if you want to be on the front lines of equipping God's people, this series will show you how!

THE MINISTER'S HANDBOOK

By Colette Toach

This is your manual on effective ministry. Whether you are dealing with an unexpected demon manifestation or you need to give marital counsel, you will find the answers here.

Colette Toach gives it to you in plain language. She gives you the steps 1, 2, 3 of how to do what God has called you to do. Keep a copy on hand, because you will come back to it time and time again!

PASTOR TEACHER SCHOOL

www.pastorteacherschool.com

The Lord had not called me to simply educate. He called me to train. To shape and equip His mighty warriors. I was not allowed any shortcuts. So my training never ended. To this day, He continues to shape and change me. With each lesson I learn, I pass it on to those He sends me.

This is the core of what you will find in the Pastor Teacher School - **Education by means of training**. An interactive experience that causes you to live and walk out the call that God has given to you.

Every lesson is practical, direct, and it... equips! Along with the knowledge, you gain experience and the steps to fulfilling your ministry right now.

There are many who are willing to sell you a book in the Church today, but not many who are willing to *train* you. This is what burns in us and if the Lord has sent you to our ministry, then that is what you can expect from us. A no-nonsense, boot camp that is designed to train you for your calling.

You bring your passion for God to the table and we will bring the anointing and skill to train you into what God has intended. **Together... we will change the world!**

- Colette Toach

Contact Information

To check out our wide selection of materials, go to: www.ami-bookshop.com

Do you have any questions about any products?

Contact us at: +1 (760) 466 - 7679
(9am to 5pm California Time, Weekdays Only)

E-mail Address: admin@ami-bookshop.com

Postal Address:

> A.M.I.
> 5663 Balboa Ave #416
> San Diego, CA 92111, USA

Facebook Page:
http://www.facebook.com/ApostolicMovementInternational

YouTube Page:
https://www.youtube.com/c/ApostolicMovementInternational

Twitter Page: https://twitter.com/apmoveint

Amazon.com Page: www.amazon.com/author/colettetoach

AMI Bookshop – It's not Just Knowledge, It's **Living Knowledge**